Canadian Living
Essential Salads

EXCLUSIVE DISTRIBUTOR FOR CANADA & USA
Simon & Schuster Canada
166 King Street East, Suite 300
Toronto ON M5A 1J3
Tel: 647-427-8882
Toll Free: 800-387-0446   **simonandschuster.ca**
Fax: 647-430-9446   **canadianliving.com/books**

Cataloguing data available from
Bibliothèque et Archives nationales du Québec.

Art director: Colin Elliott
Project editor: Tina Anson Mine

04-16

Legal deposit: 2016
Bibliothèque et Archives nationales du Québec
Library and Archives Canada

ISBN 978-1-988002-26-2

Printed in Canada

Government of Quebec – Tax credit for book publishing –
Administered by SODEC.
sodec.gouv.qc.ca

This publisher gratefully acknowledges the support of the
Société de développement des enterprises culturelles du Québec.

Canada Council   Conseil des arts
for the Arts   du Canada

We gratefully acknowledge the support of the
Canada Council for the Arts for its publishing program.

We acknowledge the financial support of our publishing activities
by the Government of Canada through the Canada Book Fund.

Canadian Living
Essential Salads

BY THE CANADIAN LIVING TEST KITCHEN

JUNIPER
PUBLISHING
A Quebecor Media Corporation

Welcome to the Canadian Living Test Kitchen

You love to cook, and we want you to feel great about every meal that comes out of your kitchen — so creating delicious, trustworthy recipes is the top priority for us in the Canadian Living Test Kitchen. We are chefs, recipe developers and food writers, all from different backgrounds but equally dedicated to the art and science of creating delicious recipes you can make right at home.

What Does Tested Till Perfect Mean?

Every year, the food specialists in the Canadian Living Test Kitchen work together to produce approximately 500 Tested-Till-Perfect recipes. So what does Tested Till Perfect mean? It means we follow a rigorous process to ensure you'll get the same results in your kitchen as we do in ours.

Here's What We Do:

- In the Test Kitchen, we use the same everyday ingredients and equipment that you use in your own kitchen.

- We start by researching ideas and brainstorming as a team.

- We write up the recipe and go straight into the kitchen to try it out.

- We taste, evaluate and tweak the recipe until we really love it.

- Each recipe then gets handed off to different food editors for another test and another tasting session.

- We meticulously test and retest each recipe as many times as it takes to make sure it turns out as perfectly in your kitchen as it does in ours.

- We carefully weigh and measure all ingredients, record the data and send the recipe out for nutritional analysis.

- The recipe is then edited and rechecked to ensure all the information is correct and it's ready for you to cook.

Our Tested-Till-Perfect guarantee means we've tested every recipe, using the same grocery store ingredients and household appliances as you do, until we're sure you'll get perfect results at home.

Endive Salad
With Herbed Goat Cheese
page 26

Contents

Salad-Building Basics

MILD GREENS

Baby greens » A variety of greens, ranging from mild-tasting lettuce to spicier mustard or beet greens.

Butterhead lettuce » Soft, pale, buttery leaves with mild flavour, such as Boston and Bibb. It's also called "butter lettuce."

Iceberg lettuce » Crisp, watery leaves with an extremely mild flavour.

Leaf lettuce » Curly, delicate leaves with a very mild flavour. Leaf lettuce comes in red and green varieties.

Mâche » Small, tender leaves with a mild, nutty, sweet flavour. Also known as lamb's lettuce or corn salad.

Romaine lettuce » Long, sturdy and crisp pale green leaves with a classic lettuce flavour. It's a must-have for Caesar salad.

Spinach » Firm, dark green leaves with an earthy but mild flavour. Baby spinach has a more delicate texture and doesn't require stemming.

SPICY OR BITTER GREENS

Arugula » Soft, dark green pepper-flavoured leaves. Baby arugula has tender stems that don't need to be trimmed.

Belgian endive » Long white to pale yellow-green leaves grown in tight, elongated heads, with a bitter flavour and a crunchy texture. It's not the same as curly endive (see frisée, below).

Escarole » Deep green, sturdy leaves in a compact head, with a bitter flavour. Young leaves are nice in salads, while more mature ones are better in soups or side dishes.

Frisée » Crisp curly-edged leaves that go from deep green outside to pale inside, with a bitter taste. It's also known as curly chicory or curly endive.

Mizuna » Tender, elongated, spiky green leaves, with a refreshing, peppery flavour. Try mizuna in any dish where you would use arugula.

Radicchio » Small heads of deep purple-red leaves with white veins, with a pleasantly bitter flavour. Radicchio is one of the few lettuces you'll see cooked—it's tasty grilled.

technique

WASHING AND STORING SALAD GREENS

1 Place the greens in a bowl or clean sink filled with cold water. Avoid running water, which can bruise delicate leaves.

2 Gently swish the greens with your hands to remove any fine grit. Let the grit settle. Lift the greens straight out of the water and place them in a salad spinner or on a clean towel.

3 Spin the greens for a few seconds, draining between rotations (if the water still looks gritty, repeat). Or gather the edges of the towel to make a bundle and shake gently.

4 Lay greens on a clean towel. Very loosely roll them up in the towel and store them in an unsealed plastic bag in the crisper drawer of the fridge. They should keep for up to a week.

TWO SALAD TOOLS WE LOVE

Salad Spinner
This gadget takes up a lot of cupboard space, but it makes washing greens and herbs easier, and dries delicate leaves without crushing them. Look for one with a large-capacity bowl, a nonskid base and a brake to stop the spinning. There are lots of different spinning mechanisms—cranks, pull cords and more—so try before you buy to see what you like.

Mandoline
The blades in these manual slicers are seriously sharp, like razors, so use care when handling them. They make quick work of slicing and julienning, and some can make fancy crinkle or waffle cuts. A studded handle comes with most; use it to hold the food against the blade and protect your fingers.

TRY ME!

Here are some exotic veggies to experiment with in salads:

Celeriac » Also known as celery root, celeriac is a large, knobby root with lots of small rootlets twisting around it. A relative of regular celery, with a vibrant celery flavour, it's tasty sliced in salads. Raw slices of celeriac oxidize quickly, so toss them with lemon juice to prevent browning.

Chayote » A type of summer squash, chayote can be thinly sliced and eaten raw, but light cooking further softens its mild taste. Chayotes are usually prepared like other summer squashes in salads and can be peeled, if desired.

Daikon radish » This large, long, white root, also called lo bok, is common in Japanese, Korean and Chinese cuisine. The flesh is tender-crisp with a pungent turnip-like aroma. The flavour is mild, however.

Kohlrabi » These small pale-green heads have a delicate broccoli-cabbage flavour. The crisp root is wonderful sliced or shredded raw for salads.

Rutabaga » Also known as swede, this large root has waxy skin covering golden flesh. In Canada, it's often served cooked and mashed like potatoes, but thin raw slices are tasty in salads.

Super Summer Whole Grain Salad
page 93

TASTY GRAINS FOR SALADS

Barley » Whole grain barley, also called pot barley, is high in fibre and pleasantly chewy in salads. Pearl barley has the bran and germ removed, so it's less nutritious but has a tender texture when cooked.

Oat groats » Oat groats are whole grains. They are tender with a firm bite when cooked, and they're great at soaking up vinaigrettes.

Quinoa » The seed of an ancient grass (not grain) plant, quinoa is gluten-free. You'll find both red and white quinoa in stores, and both are equally nutritious additions to salads.

Rice » Brown and white rice are great at absorbing dressings. Brown rice is much higher in fibre, vitamins and minerals than white rice, and it offers a chewier texture and nuttier flavour that make grain salads taste more substantial.

Rye » Whole grain rye berries (or kernels) are tasty in salads and can be substituted for wheat berries in many recipes. They have a stronger, earthier flavour than wheat berries.

Wheat » Wheat berries are packed with fibre and nutrients, and are pleasantly chewy. Spelt or kamut berries are tasty substitutes. Bulgur is a parboiled form of wheat that's great for tabbouleh.

Wild rice » This gluten-free "grain" is actually a seed from an aquatic grass that's native to Canada. The cooked kernels have a chewy texture and a nutty, slightly smoky flavour.

HINT
Oats are naturally gluten-free but can be cross-contaminated with wheat during processing. If you are avoiding gluten, buy oats that are labelled "pure uncontaminated."

Grilled Portobello Salad With Arugula

HANDS-ON TIME	•	TOTAL TIME	•	MAKES
15 MINUTES		25 MINUTES		12 SERVINGS

What you need

½ cup	walnut pieces
8	portobello mushrooms (about 450 g), stemmed and gills removed (see tip, below)
10 cups	trimmed arugula (about 2 bunches)
quarter	red onion, thinly sliced
60 g	Parmesan or Asiago cheese, shaved

ROSEMARY BALSAMIC DRESSING:

½ cup	extra-virgin olive oil
¼ cup	balsamic vinegar
1 tbsp	chopped fresh rosemary or thyme (or 1 tsp dried rosemary or thyme)
¼ tsp	each salt and pepper

How to make it

ROSEMARY BALSAMIC DRESSING: Whisk together oil, vinegar, rosemary, salt and pepper; set aside.

In dry skillet, toast walnuts over medium heat, shaking pan occasionally, until golden, about 5 minutes. Set aside.

Wipe tops of mushrooms with damp towel; cut in half. Brush with half of the dressing. Place on greased grill over medium-high heat; close lid and grill, turning once, until tender, about 10 minutes. *(Make-ahead: Let cool. Refrigerate in airtight container for up to 24 hours. Pour off any juices.)*

In large bowl, combine arugula, red onion and half of the walnuts. Add remaining dressing; toss to coat. Mound arugula mixture on platter; top with mushrooms. Sprinkle with Parmesan cheese and remaining walnuts.

TIP FROM THE TEST KITCHEN
Portobello mushroom stems can be tough. Cut them off or trim off the hardest parts if they are very short. Using a teaspoon, scrape the dark gills off the undersides of the caps. Save them for making homemade stock, if you like.

NUTRITIONAL INFORMATION, PER SERVING: about 158 cal, 5 g pro, 14 g total fat (2 g sat. fat), 6 g carb, 2 g fibre, 4 mg chol, 135 mg sodium. % RDI: 12% calcium, 8% iron, 12% vit A, 12% vit C, 25% folate.

Boston Lettuce and Mâche Salad With Buttermilk Dill Dressing

HANDS-ON TIME	TOTAL TIME	MAKES
10 MINUTES	10 MINUTES	8 SERVINGS

What you need

2	small heads Boston lettuce
4 cups	mâche, baby spinach or trimmed arugula
4	radishes, thinly sliced
1	green onion, sliced

BUTTERMILK DILL DRESSING:

⅔ cup	buttermilk
¼ cup	light mayonnaise
2 tbsp	minced fresh parsley
1 tsp	cider vinegar
½ tsp	Dijon mustard
¼ tsp	dried dillweed (see tip, below)
pinch	each salt and pepper

How to make it

BUTTERMILK DILL DRESSING: Whisk together buttermilk, mayonnaise, parsley, vinegar, mustard, dill, salt and pepper. *(Make-ahead: Refrigerate in airtight container for up to 24 hours.)*

Cut each head of Boston lettuce into quarters. Keeping lettuce wedges intact, arrange mâche between leaves. Place each wedge on salad plate; sprinkle with radishes and green onion. Drizzle with dressing.

TIP FROM THE TEST KITCHEN
You can substitute chopped fresh dill for the dried dillweed in the dressing. The general guideline is to use about three times as much of a fresh herb as you would of a dried herb. For this dressing, you'd need ¾ tsp chopped fresh dill.

NUTRITIONAL INFORMATION, PER SERVING: about 45 cal, 2 g pro, 3 g total fat (trace sat. fat), 4 g carb, 1 g fibre, 3 mg chol, 85 mg sodium. % RDI: 5% calcium, 6% iron, 25% vit A, 28% vit C, 18% folate.

Dandelion Salad
With Warm Bacon Mushroom Dressing

HANDS-ON TIME	•	TOTAL TIME	•	MAKES
20 MINUTES		25 MINUTES		4 SERVINGS

What you need

4	slices bacon
1 tbsp	extra-virgin olive oil
2 cups	oyster mushrooms, sliced
1	shallot, thinly sliced
2 tbsp	red wine vinegar
1 tsp	Dijon mustard
¼ tsp	pepper
8 cups	dandelion greens, cut in 2-inch (5 cm) lengths
4	fried eggs (see tip, below)

How to make it

In skillet, cook bacon over medium-high heat until crisp, about 6 minutes. Reserving 2 tbsp of the fat, drain bacon on paper towel–lined plate. Chop into bite-size pieces.

In same skillet, heat reserved bacon fat and oil over medium heat; cook mushrooms and shallot, stirring occasionally, until tender and golden, about 6 minutes. Remove from heat; let stand for 1 minute. Whisk in vinegar, mustard and pepper.

Place greens in large bowl; drizzle with mushroom mixture. Add bacon; toss to coat. Divide salad among 4 plates; top each with fried egg.

TIP FROM THE TEST KITCHEN

To make perfect sunny-side-up eggs, in a large nonstick skillet, melt 2 tsp of butter over medium heat. Crack 4 eggs into the pan; fry just until the whites are set, about 3 minutes. For over-easy eggs, cook them up to this point, then turn them over and fry just until a white film forms over the yolks, about 30 seconds more.

NUTRITIONAL INFORMATION, PER SERVING: about 277 cal, 13 g pro, 20 g total fat (6 g sat. fat), 13 g carb, 5 g fibre, 227 mg chol, 357 mg sodium. % RDI: 22% calcium, 36% iron, 164% vit A, 65% vit C, 28% folate.

Spicy Greens
With Maple Soy Vinaigrette

HANDS-ON TIME	•	TOTAL TIME	•	MAKES
7 MINUTES		7 MINUTES		4 SERVINGS

What you need

8 cups   loosely packed mixed greens
1   carrot, grated

MAPLE SOY VINAIGRETTE:

2 tbsp   vegetable oil
1 tbsp   unseasoned rice vinegar
2 tsp   soy sauce
2 tsp   maple syrup (see tip, below)
1 tsp   sesame oil

How to make it

MAPLE SOY VINAIGRETTE: In large bowl, whisk together vegetable oil, vinegar, soy sauce, maple syrup and sesame oil.

Add mixed greens and carrot; toss to coat.

TIP FROM THE TEST KITCHEN
Canadian maple syrup comes in three grades and five different colours. Canada No. 1 extra light and light are pale and mild; medium is also light but has a rich flavour that's perfect for this dressing. Canada No. 2 (amber) is darker, with a strong flavour that is great for cooking. Canada No. 3 (dark) is very dark with a strong, molasses-like flavour.

NUTRITIONAL INFORMATION, PER SERVING: about 107 cal, 2 g pro, 8 g total fat (1 g sat. fat), 8 g carb, 2 g fibre, 0 mg chol, 191 mg sodium, 400 mg potassium. % RDI: 7% calcium, 6% iron, 48% vit A, 27% vit C, 44% folate.

Asparagus and Mixed Greens Salad

HANDS-ON TIME	•	TOTAL TIME	•	MAKES
20 MINUTES		25 MINUTES		8 SERVINGS

What you need

1 cup	pecan pieces
1	bunch (450 g) asparagus, trimmed (see tip, below)
2 tsp	olive oil
pinch	each salt and pepper
4 cups	torn frisée
4 cups	baby arugula
4 cups	trimmed watercress
1	head Boston lettuce, torn

LEMON FENNEL VINAIGRETTE:

¼ cup	olive oil
3 tbsp	minced shallot
3 tbsp	lemon juice
2 tsp	Dijon mustard
2 tsp	liquid honey
1½ tsp	crushed fennel seeds
½ tsp	each salt and pepper

How to make it

LEMON FENNEL VINAIGRETTE: Whisk together oil, shallot, lemon juice, mustard, honey, fennel seeds, salt and pepper. Set aside. (*Make-ahead: Refrigerate in airtight container for up to 3 days. Shake or whisk to combine.*)

Bake pecans on rimmed baking sheet in 350°F (180°C) oven until lightly toasted, about 8 minutes. Let cool. (*Make-ahead: Store in airtight container for up to 5 days.*)

Toss together asparagus, oil, salt and pepper. Bake on rimmed baking sheet in 350°F (180°C) oven until tender-crisp, 6 to 8 minutes. Let cool; cover and refrigerate until cold. (*Make-ahead: Refrigerate in airtight container for up to 24 hours.*)

Arrange asparagus on salad plates. In large bowl, toss pecans, frisée, arugula, watercress, Boston lettuce and vinaigrette; divide over asparagus. Serve immediately.

TIP FROM THE TEST KITCHEN

You can use a knife to trim off the tough, woody ends of asparagus spears, but it's just as easy to snap them off. Hold the end and the middle of the spear and bend until the end snaps off. If you don't want to waste the ends, save them for making asparagus soup (simply purée and strain out the fibrous bits).

NUTRITIONAL INFORMATION, PER SERVING: about 200 cal, 4 g pro, 18 g total fat (2 g sat. fat), 9 g carb, 4 g fibre, 0 mg chol, 188 mg sodium, 458 mg potassium. % RDI: 10% calcium, 13% iron, 28% vit A, 32% vit C, 65% folate.

Harvest Salad

HANDS-ON TIME	•	TOTAL TIME	•	MAKES
15 MINUTES		35 MINUTES		8 SERVINGS

What you need

3 cups	cubed pumpernickel or rye bread
1	pkg (115 g) mâche or mixed baby greens
3	heads Belgian endive, separated into leaves
115 g	blue cheese, crumbled
2	hard-cooked eggs (see tip, below), quartered
1	apple, cored and cut in chunks
½ cup	walnut halves

CARAWAY DRESSING:

2 tsp	caraway seeds
⅓ cup	finely chopped shallots or onion
3 tbsp	white wine vinegar
¼ tsp	salt
1 tbsp	Dijon mustard
1	clove garlic, minced
¼ tsp	white pepper
⅓ cup	extra-virgin olive oil

How to make it

Bake bread cubes on rimmed baking sheet in 350°F (180°C) oven until crisp, about 10 minutes. Transfer to large bowl.

CARAWAY DRESSING: Meanwhile, in small dry skillet, toast caraway seeds over medium-low heat until fragrant, about 2 minutes. Let cool slightly. In mortar with pestle or using bottom of heavy pot, crush caraway seeds.

In small bowl, combine shallots, vinegar and salt; let stand for 5 minutes. Stir in mustard, garlic, pepper and caraway seeds; whisk in oil.

To bowl with croutons, add mâche, Belgian endive, blue cheese, eggs, apple and walnuts. Pour dressing over top; toss to coat.

TIP FROM THE TEST KITCHEN

Here's our foolproof method for making hard-cooked eggs: Arrange eggs in a single layer in a saucepan and pour in enough cold water to cover them by 1 inch (2.5 cm). Cover and bring them to a boil. Remove the pan from the heat and let it stand for 12 minutes. Drain and chill the eggs under cold water. Drain and peel off the shells.

NUTRITIONAL INFORMATION, PER SERVING: about 246 cal, 8 g pro, 19 g total fat (5 g sat. fat), 13 g carb, 3 g fibre, 57 mg chol, 399 mg sodium, 268 mg potassium. % RDI: 11% calcium, 10% iron, 16% vit A, 13% vit C, 17% folate.

Greek-Style Romaine Salad

HANDS-ON TIME	**TOTAL TIME**	**MAKES**
10 MINUTES	10 MINUTES	4 TO 6 SERVINGS

What you need

4 cups	torn romaine lettuce
1 cup	cherry tomatoes, quartered
1 cup	cubed English cucumber
half	sweet green pepper, chopped
⅓ cup	sliced red onion
¼ cup	crumbled feta cheese
8	Kalamata olives

GARLIC AND OREGANO DRESSING:

2 tbsp	extra-virgin olive oil
1 tbsp	red wine vinegar
1	small clove garlic, minced
¼ tsp	dried oregano
pinch	pepper

How to make it

GARLIC AND OREGANO DRESSING: In glass measure, whisk together oil, vinegar, garlic, oregano and pepper; set aside.

In large bowl, toss together lettuce, tomatoes, cucumber, green pepper and red onion. Drizzle dressing over top; toss to coat. Sprinkle with feta cheese and olives.

TIP FROM THE TEST KITCHEN
Although traditional Greek salad — also called village salad — doesn't contain lettuce, we've added it to this recipe to give the dish a little more substance and textural contrast.

NUTRITIONAL INFORMATION, PER EACH OF 6 SERVINGS:
about 86 cal, 2 g pro, 7 g total fat (2 g sat. fat), 5 g carb, 2 g fibre, 6 mg chol, 180 mg sodium. % RDI: 5% calcium, 5% iron, 22% vit A, 32% vit C, 24% folate.

Warm Pear and Hazelnut Salad

HANDS-ON TIME	TOTAL TIME	MAKES
10 MINUTES	10 MINUTES	4 SERVINGS

What you need

1 tbsp	butter
2	firm ripe pears (such as Bartlett), cored and cut in ¼-inch (5 mm) thick slices
3 tbsp	sherry vinegar
1 tbsp	packed brown sugar
3 tbsp	olive oil
1 tsp	Dijon mustard
1 tsp	liquid honey
¼ tsp	each salt and pepper
12 cups	baby arugula
100 g	Cambozola cheese, broken in chunks
¼ cup	skinned toasted hazelnuts (see tip, below)

How to make it

In skillet, melt butter over medium-high heat; cook pears for 1 minute. Add 1 tbsp of the vinegar and brown sugar; toss to coat. Cook until fork-tender, about 2 minutes.

Meanwhile, in large bowl, whisk together remaining vinegar, oil, mustard, honey, salt and pepper. Toss with arugula. Divide among 4 plates; sprinkle with Cambozola cheese, hazelnuts and warm pears.

VARIATION

Warm Apple and Hazelnut Salad
Substitute baby spinach for the arugula, and tart apples for the pears.

TIP FROM THE TEST KITCHEN
Toast hazelnuts in a single layer on a rimmed baking sheet in a 350°F (180°C) oven until they're fragrant and the skins crack, about 10 minutes. Let them cool slightly. Transfer the nuts to a tea towel and briskly rub them to remove the skins. Pick the skinned nuts off the towel and they're ready to use.

NUTRITIONAL INFORMATION, PER SERVING: about 365 cal, 7 g pro, 29 g total fat (10 g sat. fat), 22 g carb, 5 g fibre, 37 mg chol, 551 mg sodium, 416 mg potassium. % RDI: 23% calcium, 12% iron, 27% vit A, 20% vit C, 35% folate.

Kohlrabi, Red Apple and Walnut Salad

HANDS-ON TIME	•	TOTAL TIME	•	MAKES
20 MINUTES		35 MINUTES		6 SERVINGS

What you need

½ cup	walnut pieces
85 g	blue cheese, crumbled
⅓ cup	0% plain Greek yogurt
2 tbsp	lemon juice
1 tbsp	milk
2 tbsp	thinly sliced fresh chives
dash	hot pepper sauce
pinch	each salt and pepper
1	red-skinned apple
2	kohlrabi, trimmed, peeled, halved and thinly sliced in half-moons
6 cups	baby arugula

How to make it

Toast walnuts on rimmed baking sheet in 350°F (180°C) oven until light golden, 6 to 8 minutes. Let cool.

Set aside 2 tbsp of the blue cheese for garnish. In bowl, combine remaining blue cheese, yogurt, 1 tbsp of the lemon juice and milk, mashing with fork until almost smooth. Stir in chives, hot pepper sauce, salt and pepper; set dressing aside.

Cut apple in half; core and thinly slice. In large bowl, toss apple with remaining lemon juice. Add kohlrabi and arugula; toss with dressing to coat. Garnish with walnuts and reserved blue cheese.

NUTRITIONAL INFORMATION, PER SERVING: about 150 cal, 7 g pro, 11 g total fat (3 g sat. fat), 9 g carb, 3 g fibre, 12 mg chol, 218 mg sodium, 283 mg potassium. % RDI: 15% calcium, 6% iron, 9% vit A, 38% vit C, 19% folate.

Endive and Apple Salad With Fried Camembert

HANDS-ON TIME	•	TOTAL TIME	•	MAKES
20 MINUTES		20 MINUTES		4 TO 6 SERVINGS

What you need

4 cups	chopped Belgian endive
4 cups	mâche or trimmed watercress
1	red-skinned apple, quartered, cored and thinly sliced
½ cup	thinly sliced sweet onion
1	round (about 370 g) Camembert cheese
¼ cup	all-purpose flour
1	egg, beaten
1¼ cups	fine fresh bread crumbs
	vegetable oil for frying

CIDER DIJON VINAIGRETTE:

2 tbsp	cider vinegar
2 tsp	Dijon mustard
pinch	each salt and pepper
2 tbsp	vegetable oil
2 tbsp	extra-virgin olive oil

How to make it

CIDER DIJON VINAIGRETTE: In small bowl, whisk together vinegar, mustard, salt and pepper; whisk in vegetable oil and olive oil.

In large bowl, combine Belgian endive, mâche, apple and onion. Set salad and vinaigrette aside.

Cut Camembert cheese into 4 to 6 wedges. Place flour, egg and bread crumbs in separate shallow bowls. Coat each cheese wedge in flour, gently shaking off excess; dip in egg, letting excess drip back into dish. Dip again in flour, then in egg. Coat with bread crumbs, pressing to cover completely.

In skillet, pour in enough oil to come ½ inch (1 cm) up side; heat over medium-high heat. Fry cheese, turning once, until golden, 1 to 2 minutes per side. Drain on paper towel–lined plate.

Toss Belgian endive mixture with vinaigrette; divide among plates. Top each with cheese wedge.

TIP FROM THE TEST KITCHEN
Divided into four servings, this salad is a delicious main dish; divided into six servings, it's an elegant first course.

NUTRITIONAL INFORMATION, PER EACH OF 6 SERVINGS: about 380 cal, 16 g pro, 29 g total fat (11 g sat. fat), 16 g carb, 3 g fibre, 75 mg chol, 609 mg sodium, 390 mg potassium. % RDI: 27% calcium, 8% iron, 28% vit A, 22% vit C, 40% folate.

Endive Salad
With Herbed Goat Cheese

HANDS-ON TIME	·	TOTAL TIME	·	MAKES
10 MINUTES		30 MINUTES		6 SERVINGS

What you need

2 tbsp	each chopped fresh chives and fresh parsley
½ tsp	herbes de Provence or dried thyme
1	log (113 g) soft goat cheese
6 cups	torn mixed greens
18	leaves Belgian endive (about 1 large head)

CROÛTES:

1	baguette
half	clove garlic
2 tsp	extra-virgin olive oil
¼ tsp	sea salt or salt
¼ tsp	pepper

LEMON VINAIGRETTE:

3 tbsp	vegetable oil
2 tsp	lemon juice
½ tsp	Dijon mustard
¼ tsp	granulated sugar
pinch	each salt and pepper

How to make it

CROÛTES: Cut baguette into twelve ½-inch (1 cm) thick slices; rub 1 side of each with cut side of garlic. Brush with oil; sprinkle with salt and pepper. Bake on rimmed baking sheet in 350°F (180°C) oven until crisp and light golden, about 8 minutes. Let cool. *(Make-ahead: Store in airtight container for up to 24 hours.)*

LEMON VINAIGRETTE: Whisk together oil, lemon juice, mustard, sugar, salt and pepper. *(Make-ahead: Cover and refrigerate for up to 24 hours.)*

On waxed paper, combine chives, parsley and herbes de Provence; roll goat cheese in herb mixture to coat. *(Make-ahead: Wrap in plastic wrap and refrigerate for up to 24 hours.)*

Toss mixed greens with vinaigrette; arrange on 6 plates. Top each salad with 3 Belgian endive leaves. Cut goat cheese into 6 slices; place 1 slice on each salad. Add 2 croûtes to each plate.

NUTRITIONAL INFORMATION, PER SERVING: about 292 cal, 9 g pro, 17 g total fat (4 g sat. fat), 27 g carb, 3 g fibre, 9 mg chol, 438 mg sodium. % RDI: 10% calcium, 16% iron, 19% vit A, 18% vit C, 41% folate.

Mandarin Spinach Salad

HANDS-ON TIME	TOTAL TIME	MAKES
10 MINUTES	10 MINUTES	4 SERVINGS

What you need

2 tbsp	vegetable oil
1 tbsp	unseasoned rice vinegar
1 tsp	grainy mustard
pinch	each salt and pepper
4 cups	baby spinach
½ cup	bean sprouts
¼ cup	sliced almonds (optional), toasted (see tip, below)
3	radishes, thinly sliced
1	green onion, sliced
1	can (284 mL) mandarin oranges, drained and patted dry

How to make it

In large bowl, whisk together oil, vinegar, grainy mustard, salt and pepper.

Add spinach, bean sprouts, almonds (if using), radishes, green onion and mandarin oranges; toss to coat.

TIP FROM THE TEST KITCHEN

Watch sliced and slivered almonds carefully as they toast; they can burn quickly. Toasting them in a dry skillet over medium-high heat on the stove is the easiest way to keep an eye on them. Shake the pan constantly, and take the nuts off the heat immediately when they're golden and fragrant. Transfer them to a bowl so they don't cook further.

NUTRITIONAL INFORMATION, PER SERVING: about 93 cal, 2 g pro, 7 g total fat (1 g sat. fat), 7 g carb, 2 g fibre, 0 mg chol, 43 mg sodium. % RDI: 4% calcium, 9% iron, 35% vit A, 47% vit C, 33% folate.

Bitter Greens Salad

HANDS-ON TIME	TOTAL TIME	MAKES
10 MINUTES	10 MINUTES	6 TO 8 SERVINGS

What you need

4 cups	torn Boston lettuce
4 cups	torn radicchio
2 cups	sliced Belgian endive
2 cups	torn escarole or frisée
1	green onion, sliced
⅓ cup	extra-virgin olive oil
¼ cup	wine vinegar, cider vinegar or fruit vinegar (see tip, below)
¼ tsp	sea salt or salt
¼ tsp	pepper

How to make it

In large bowl, toss together Boston lettuce, radicchio, Belgian endive, escarole and green onion.

Sprinkle lettuce mixture with oil, vinegar, salt and pepper; toss to coat.

TIP FROM THE TEST KITCHEN
Farmer's markets are good places to buy fruit vinegars. Raspberry, cranberry, blueberry or blackberry would all work well in this dressing.

NUTRITIONAL INFORMATION, PER EACH OF 8 SERVINGS:
about 93 cal, 1 g pro, 9 g total fat (1 g sat. fat), 3 g carb, 1 g fibre, 0 mg chol, 58 mg sodium. % RDI: 2% calcium, 3% iron, 6% vit A, 10% vit C, 21% folate.

Sun-Dried Tomato Vinaigrette

**MAKES
ABOUT 1 CUP**

What you need

¼ cup	drained oil-packed sun-dried tomatoes
2 tbsp	balsamic vinegar
1	clove garlic, minced
1 tsp	dried oregano
½ tsp	granulated sugar
¼ tsp	pepper
pinch	salt (optional)
⅓ cup	extra-virgin olive oil

How to make it

Rinse sun-dried tomatoes; pat dry. Finely chop and place in small bowl; whisk in ½ cup water, vinegar, garlic, oregano, sugar, pepper, and salt (if using).

Whisking constantly, drizzle in oil in slow steady stream until combined. *(Make-ahead: Refrigerate in airtight container for up to 5 days.)*

NUTRITIONAL INFORMATION, PER 1 TBSP: about 71 cal, trace pro, 5 g total fat (1 g sat. fat), 7 g carb, trace fibre, 0 mg chol, 5 mg sodium. % RDI: 1% iron, 3% vit C.

Oregano Red Wine Vinaigrette

**MAKES
ABOUT 1 CUP**

What you need

⅓ cup	extra-virgin olive oil
⅓ cup	vegetable oil
3 tbsp	red wine vinegar
2 tsp	Dijon mustard
1	clove garlic, minced
1 tsp	dried oregano
½ tsp	each salt and pepper

How to make it

In bowl, whisk together olive oil, vegetable oil, vinegar, 2 tbsp water, mustard, garlic, oregano, salt and pepper. *(Make-ahead: Refrigerate in airtight container for up to 5 days.)*

NUTRITIONAL INFORMATION, PER 1 TBSP: about 81 cal, 0 g pro, 9 g total fat (1 g sat. fat), trace carb, 0 g fibre, 0 mg chol, 80 mg sodium. % RDI: 1% iron.

Cranberry Shallot Vinaigrette

**MAKES
ABOUT 1 CUP**

What you need

½ cup	frozen cranberry concentrate, thawed
¼ cup	vegetable oil
¼ cup	red wine vinegar
2 tsp	grainy mustard
2	shallots, minced
½ tsp	each salt and pepper

How to make it

In bowl, whisk together cranberry concentrate, ¼ cup water, oil, vinegar, mustard, shallots, salt and pepper. *(Make-ahead: Refrigerate in airtight container for up to 5 days.)*

NUTRITIONAL INFORMATION, PER 1 TBSP: about 51 cal, trace pro, 3 g total fat (trace sat. fat), 5 g carb, trace fibre, 0 mg chol, 81 mg sodium, 11 mg potassium. % RDI: 1% iron, 7% vit C.

Smoky Green Salad
With Creamy Almond Dressing

HANDS-ON TIME	•	TOTAL TIME	•	MAKES
20 MINUTES		20 MINUTES		8 SERVINGS

What you need

4	slices double-smoked bacon or regular bacon
1	head red leaf lettuce, torn
6 cups	lightly packed trimmed spinach
115 g	smoked Gouda cheese, cubed
2 cups	thinly sliced cremini mushrooms
3 tbsp	toasted pepitas (see tip, page 124)

CREAMY ALMOND DRESSING:

3 tbsp	almond butter
2 tbsp	sherry vinegar or red wine vinegar
2 tbsp	light-tasting olive oil or vegetable oil
1 tbsp	liquid honey
¼ tsp	each smoked paprika and pepper
pinch	salt

How to make it

In large skillet, cook bacon over medium heat, turning once, until crisp, 5 to 8 minutes. Drain on paper towel–lined plate.

In large bowl, combine lettuce, spinach, Gouda cheese, mushrooms and pepitas.

CREAMY ALMOND DRESSING: Whisk together almond butter, vinegar, oil, 2 tbsp water, honey, paprika, pepper and salt until smooth.

Pour dressing over salad; toss to coat. Crumble bacon over top.

TIP FROM THE TEST KITCHEN
Double-smoked bacon is cured, unlike regular bacon, which is brined. It's also smoked for more than twice as long as regular bacon, giving it a rich, intensely smoky flavour.

NUTRITIONAL INFORMATION, PER SERVING: about 176 cal, 8 g pro, 14 g total fat (4 g sat. fat), 7 g carb, 1 g fibre, 20 mg chol, 219 mg sodium, 387 mg potassium. % RDI: 14% calcium, 14% iron, 53% vit A, 13% vit C, 31% folate.

Pea, Fennel and Goat Cheese Salad

HANDS-ON TIME		TOTAL TIME		MAKES
10 MINUTES	•	10 MINUTES	•	4 SERVINGS

What you need

1½ cups	shelled fresh peas
6 cups	lightly packed baby spinach
1	bulb fennel, cored and thinly sliced
⅓ cup	crumbled soft goat cheese

DRESSING:

2 tbsp	extra-virgin olive oil
1 tbsp	lemon juice
pinch	each salt and pepper
pinch	granulated sugar

How to make it

In saucepan of boiling salted water, cook peas until tender-crisp, about 2 minutes. Drain and pat dry; set aside.

DRESSING: In large bowl, whisk together oil, lemon juice, salt, pepper and sugar.

Add spinach, fennel and peas; gently toss to coat. Sprinkle with goat cheese.

TIP FROM THE TEST KITCHEN

When fresh peas are out of season, make this salad with frozen peas. Cook them just until they're heated through.

NUTRITIONAL INFORMATION, PER SERVING: about 166 cal, 7 g pro, 10 g total fat (3 g sat. fat), 14 g carb, 6 g fibre, 6 mg chol, 238 mg sodium, 642 mg potassium. % RDI: 10% calcium, 19% iron, 51% vit A, 46% vit C, 63% folate.

Radicchio and Arugula Salad With Goat Cheese and Pears

HANDS-ON TIME	•	TOTAL TIME	•	MAKES
15 MINUTES		15 MINUTES		8 SERVINGS

What you need

2	heads radicchio, torn
4 cups	lightly packed baby arugula
half	red onion, thinly sliced
1	pear, cored and cut in thin wedges
15	pitted prunes, halved
¾ cup	toasted pecan pieces (see tip, below)
3 tbsp	finely chopped fresh chives
115 g	soft goat cheese, crumbled (about 1 cup)

GRAINY MUSTARD DRESSING:

2 tbsp	red wine vinegar
2 tbsp	extra-virgin olive oil
4 tsp	grainy mustard
¼ tsp	each salt and pepper
pinch	granulated sugar

How to make it

In large bowl, toss together radicchio, arugula, red onion, pear, prunes, pecans and chives.

GRAINY MUSTARD DRESSING: Whisk together vinegar, oil, mustard, salt, pepper and sugar.

Pour dressing over salad; toss to coat. Sprinkle with goat cheese.

TIP FROM THE TEST KITCHEN

To toast pecans, spread them in a single layer on a rimmed baking sheet; toast in a 325°F (160°C) oven until they are fragrant, 4 to 6 minutes. For small amounts, toast them in a skillet over medium heat, shaking often, for 3 to 5 minutes.

NUTRITIONAL INFORMATION, PER SERVING: about 212 cal, 5 g pro, 14 g total fat (3 g sat. fat), 19 g carb, 4 g fibre, 7 mg chol, 170 mg sodium, 391 mg potassium. % RDI: 6% calcium, 11% iron, 10% vit A, 12% vit C, 21% folate.

Roasted Beet and Feta Salad

HANDS-ON TIME	TOTAL TIME	MAKES
20 MINUTES	1¼ HOURS	4 SERVINGS

What you need

6	baby beets, trimmed
3 tbsp	extra-virgin olive oil
2 tbsp	red wine vinegar
½ tsp	Dijon mustard
pinch	each salt and pepper
6 cups	loosely packed baby greens
¼ cup	thinly sliced red onion
2 tbsp	chopped fresh parsley
2 tbsp	chopped fresh dill
2 tbsp	chopped fresh chives
½ cup	crumbled feta cheese

How to make it

Wrap beets in double-thickness square of foil; roast on baking sheet in 425°F (220°C) oven until tender, about 45 minutes. Let cool enough to handle. Remove skins; cut beets into wedges. Set aside.

In large bowl, whisk together oil, vinegar, mustard, salt and pepper. Add greens, red onion, parsley, dill, chives and beets; toss to coat. Sprinkle with feta cheese.

TIP FROM THE TEST KITCHEN
Baby beets are tender and less fibrous than fully grown beets. They're the best choice for this salad.

NUTRITIONAL INFORMATION, PER SERVING: about 184 cal, 5 g pro, 15 g total fat (4 g sat. fat), 10 g carb, 3 g fibre, 17 mg chol, 287 mg sodium, 466 mg potassium. % RDI: 15% calcium, 11% iron, 23% vit A, 30% vit C, 59% folate.

Vegetarian Chef's Salad

HANDS-ON TIME	TOTAL TIME	MAKES
15 MINUTES	15 MINUTES	4 SERVINGS

What you need

6 cups	torn iceberg lettuce
2 cups	torn radicchio
½ cup	alfalfa sprouts (about half 35 g pkg)
4	radishes, thinly sliced
¾ cup	sliced English cucumber
⅓ cup	thinly sliced sweet onion
½ cup	rinsed drained canned chickpeas
3	hard-cooked eggs (see tip, page 19), quartered
1	large tomato, cut in 12 wedges
half	avocado, pitted, peeled and sliced
60 g	each Swiss and Cheddar cheeses, cut in sticks

PICKLE AND CAPER DRESSING:

¼ cup	light mayonnaise
1 tbsp	minced dill pickle
1 tbsp	extra-virgin olive oil
2 tsp	tomato-based chili sauce
1½ tsp	lemon juice
½ tsp	capers, drained and minced
½ tsp	Dijon mustard
pinch	each salt and pepper

How to make it

PICKLE AND CAPER DRESSING: In small bowl, stir together mayonnaise, dill pickle, oil, chili sauce, lemon juice, capers, mustard, salt and pepper.

In large bowl, toss together iceberg lettuce, radicchio, sprouts, radishes, cucumber, onion and half of the dressing; arrange on 4 large plates.

Top with chickpeas, eggs, tomato, avocado, and Swiss and Cheddar cheeses; spoon remaining dressing over top.

NUTRITIONAL INFORMATION, PER SERVING: about 349 cal, 16 g pro, 25 g total fat (9 g sat. fat), 17 g carb, 5 g fibre, 173 mg chol, 430 mg sodium. % RDI: 25% calcium, 14% iron, 20% vit A, 32% vit C, 60% folate.

Oven-Poached Salmon Salad With Mustard Vinaigrette

HANDS-ON TIME	•	TOTAL TIME	•	MAKES
15 MINUTES		25 MINUTES		4 SERVINGS

What you need

4	skinless centre-cut salmon fillets (each about 175 g), see tip, below
¼ tsp	each salt and pepper
1 tbsp	capers, drained and rinsed
1	lemon, thinly sliced
4	sprigs fresh thyme
450 g	new potatoes, scrubbed and halved
450 g	green beans
1 cup	grape tomatoes
6 cups	torn romaine lettuce
4	hard-cooked eggs (see tip, page 19), quartered

MUSTARD VINAIGRETTE:

3 tbsp	extra-virgin olive oil
1 tbsp	white wine vinegar
2 tsp	lemon juice
2 tsp	Dijon mustard
1	shallot or green onion (white part only), minced
1 tsp	minced fresh thyme
¼ tsp	each salt and pepper
pinch	granulated sugar

How to make it

MUSTARD VINAIGRETTE: In large bowl, whisk together oil, vinegar, lemon juice, mustard, shallot, thyme, salt, pepper and sugar; set aside.

Place fish in centre of large piece of parchment paper. Sprinkle with salt and pepper; top with capers, lemon and thyme. Fold paper over fish so edges match; double-fold and pinch all edges to seal packet. Roast on baking sheet in 450°F (230°C) oven until fish flakes easily when tested, 10 to 15 minutes.

Meanwhile, in saucepan of boiling salted water, cook potatoes until almost fork-tender, about 8 minutes.

Add beans; cook until tender, about 2 minutes. Drain and rinse under cold water; pat dry. Add to vinaigrette along with tomatoes; toss to coat.

Arrange lettuce on plates. Top with potato mixture, eggs and salmon; drizzle with any remaining vinaigrette.

TIP FROM THE TEST KITCHEN
Go ahead and buy skin-on salmon fillets if you don't mind skinning the fish yourself.

NUTRITIONAL INFORMATION, PER SERVING: about 575 cal, 41 g pro, 32 g total fat (6 g sat. fat), 32 g carb, 7 g fibre, 270 mg chol, 978 mg sodium, 1,344 mg potassium. % RDI: 12% calcium, 25% iron, 59% vit A, 88% vit C, 96% folate.

Updated Chicken Caesar

HANDS-ON TIME	TOTAL TIME	MAKES
15 MINUTES	30 MINUTES	4 SERVINGS

What you need

4	boneless skinless chicken breasts (450 g)
4 tsp	extra-virgin olive oil
2 tsp	Montreal Steak Spice (see tip, below)
2	romaine lettuce hearts
⅓ cup	shaved Parmesan cheese

CAESAR VINAIGRETTE:

1½ tsp	grated lemon zest
¼ cup	lemon juice
¼ cup	extra-virgin olive oil
3 tbsp	red wine vinegar
4	anchovy fillets, minced
1	clove garlic, minced
pinch	each salt and pepper

How to make it

Toss chicken with half of the oil and the Montreal Steak Spice; let stand for 10 minutes.

In large skillet, heat remaining oil over medium-high heat; cook chicken, turning once, until golden and no longer pink inside, 8 to 10 minutes. Let stand for 5 minutes; thinly slice crosswise.

Meanwhile, trim root end of each romaine heart, leaving core intact. Quarter each heart lengthwise through core.

CAESAR VINAIGRETTE: Whisk together lemon zest, lemon juice, oil, red wine vinegar, anchovies, garlic, salt and pepper.

Arrange 2 of the romaine quarters on each of 4 plates; top with chicken. Drizzle with vinaigrette; sprinkle with Parmesan cheese.

TIP FROM THE TEST KITCHEN
Montreal Steak Spice is a trademarked name for a blend of herbs and spices typically used to season steak and other meats. It's a mix of black and red pepper, salt, garlic, onion, dill, mustard and herbs. Look for it in the spice aisle of the supermarket and in bulk stores.

NUTRITIONAL INFORMATION, PER SERVING: about 406 cal, 38 g pro, 23 g total fat (4 g sat. fat), 13 g carb, 7 g fibre, 87 mg chol, 479 mg sodium, 1,200 mg potassium. % RDI: 18% calcium, 29% iron, 274% vit A, 138% vit C, 196% folate.

Grilled Buffalo Chicken Salad With Blue Cheese Dressing

HANDS-ON TIME	TOTAL TIME	MAKES
25 MINUTES	25 MINUTES	4 SERVINGS

What you need

8 cups	torn leaf lettuce
1 cup	sliced English cucumber
1	small carrot, shredded

GRILLED BUFFALO CHICKEN:

¼ cup	cayenne pepper–based hot sauce (such as Frank's RedHot)
2 tbsp	butter, melted
450 g	boneless skinless chicken cutlets

BLUE CHEESE DRESSING:

⅓ cup	buttermilk
¼ cup	crumbled blue cheese
3 tbsp	2% plain yogurt
1 tbsp	cider vinegar
¼ tsp	granulated sugar
pinch	pepper

How to make it

GRILLED BUFFALO CHICKEN: Stir hot sauce with butter; remove 2 tbsp and set aside. Place chicken on greased grill over medium-high heat; close lid and grill, brushing with remaining sauce and turning once, until chicken is no longer pink inside, about 8 minutes. Let stand for 5 minutes; slice chicken and toss with reserved sauce.

BLUE CHEESE DRESSING: Meanwhile, whisk together buttermilk, blue cheese, yogurt, vinegar, sugar and pepper until combined.

Divide lettuce, cucumber and carrot among 4 plates. Top with chicken; drizzle with dressing.

NUTRITIONAL INFORMATION, PER SERVING: about 219 cal, 30 g pro, 7 g total fat (4 g sat. fat), 7 g carb, 2 g fibre, 83 mg chol, 486 mg sodium, 629 mg potassium. % RDI: 12% calcium, 9% iron, 78% vit A, 25% vit C, 18% folate.

Grilled Chicken Club Salad

HANDS-ON TIME	•	TOTAL TIME	•	MAKES
25 MINUTES		1 HOUR		6 SERVINGS

What you need

750 g	boneless skinless chicken breasts
half	red onion
12	slices bacon
24	cherry tomatoes
pinch	each salt and pepper
6 cups	torn romaine lettuce
1½ cups	croutons (such as Parmesan Croutons, page 52)

CREAMY HERBED DRESSING:

2 tbsp	minced fresh parsley
2 tbsp	light mayonnaise
2 tbsp	white wine vinegar
4 tsp	grainy or Dijon mustard
½ tsp	dried basil
¼ tsp	each salt and pepper
⅔ cup	vegetable oil

How to make it

CREAMY HERBED DRESSING: In small bowl, whisk together parsley, mayonnaise, vinegar, mustard, basil, salt and pepper; slowly whisk in oil until emulsified. *(Make-ahead: Cover and refrigerate for up to 4 days.)*

Cut chicken into thirty-six 1-inch (2.5 cm) cubes; place in bowl. Add half of the dressing; toss to coat. Cover and refrigerate for 30 minutes.

Cut red onion into twenty-four 1½-inch (4 cm) pieces. Cut each bacon slice crosswise into thirds. Wrap 1 bacon piece around each chicken cube. Onto each of 12 metal or soaked 10-inch (25 cm) wooden skewers, thread 1 chicken cube, 1 piece red onion and 1 tomato. Repeat once. Finish with 1 chicken cube. Sprinkle with salt and pepper.

Place skewers on greased grill over medium heat; close lid and grill, turning 3 times, until bacon is crisp and chicken is no longer pink inside, about 12 minutes.

Mound lettuce and croutons on 6 plates; top each with 2 skewers. Drizzle with remaining dressing.

NUTRITIONAL INFORMATION, PER SERVING: about 435 cal, 32 g pro, 28 g total fat (4 g sat. fat), 13 g carb, 2 g fibre, 78 mg chol, 462 mg sodium. % RDI: 4% calcium, 15% iron, 19% vit A, 47% vit C, 45% folate.

Crispy Tortilla Ancho Chicken Salad

HANDS-ON TIME	•	TOTAL TIME	•	MAKES
15 MINUTES		15 MINUTES		4 SERVINGS

What you need

3	small flour tortillas, halved and cut crosswise in ½-inch (1 cm) wide strips
1 tbsp	vegetable oil
450 g	boneless skinless chicken breasts, cut in ¾-inch (2 cm) cubes
1	sweet red pepper, chopped
2	cloves garlic, minced
1¼ tsp	ancho chili powder (see tip, below)
¼ tsp	pepper
pinch	salt
1 cup	rinsed drained canned black beans
½ cup	frozen corn kernels
2	green onions, chopped
1 tbsp	lime juice
4 cups	torn leaf lettuce
½ cup	shredded old Cheddar cheese
1	avocado, pitted, peeled and chopped

HONEY LIME DRESSING:

3 tbsp	olive oil
2 tbsp	lime juice
2 tsp	liquid honey
pinch	salt

How to make it

Toss tortilla strips with 1 tsp of the oil. In large nonstick skillet, cook strips over medium-high heat, tossing often, until golden, about 2 minutes. Transfer to bowl.

Add remaining oil to skillet; cook chicken, red pepper, garlic, chili powder, pepper and salt, stirring often, until chicken is no longer pink inside, about 4 minutes.

Stir in beans, corn, green onions and lime juice; cook until warmed through, about 3 minutes.

HONEY LIME DRESSING: In large bowl, whisk together oil, lime juice, honey and salt.

Add lettuce to dressing; toss to coat. Spoon chicken mixture over lettuce mixture; sprinkle with Cheddar cheese and avocado. Garnish with tortilla strips.

TIP FROM THE TEST KITCHEN
Ancho chili powder has a mildly spicy edge. Substitute regular mild chili powder if you prefer it.

NUTRITIONAL INFORMATION, PER SERVING: about 539 cal, 36 g pro, 29 g total fat (6 g sat. fat), 35 g carb, 9 g fibre, 81 mg chol, 496 mg sodium, 958 mg potassium. % RDI: 14% calcium, 22% iron, 36% vit A, 63% vit C, 56% folate.

Apricot, Chicken and Almond Salad

| HANDS-ON TIME | | TOTAL TIME | | MAKES |
| 10 MINUTES | • | 10 MINUTES | • | 2 SERVINGS |

What you need

2 tbsp	olive oil (approx)
2	boneless skinless chicken breasts
2 tsp	balsamic vinegar
pinch	each salt and pepper
2 cups	torn Boston lettuce
⅓ cup	cubed feta cheese (see tip, below)
⅓ cup	chopped dried apricots
¼ cup	sliced almonds, toasted (see tip, page 27)

How to make it

Brush nonstick skillet lightly with oil; heat over medium-high heat. Cook chicken, turning once, until no longer pink inside, 10 to 12 minutes. Let cool; dice. Transfer to large bowl.

Whisk together remaining 2 tbsp oil, vinegar, salt and pepper until well combined.

Add lettuce, feta cheese, apricots and almonds to chicken. Drizzle dressing over top; toss to coat.

TIP FROM THE TEST KITCHEN
Cow's milk feta is softer, creamier and a bit more sour than Greek or Bulgarian feta, both of which are predominantly made from sheep's milk.

NUTRITIONAL INFORMATION, PER SERVING: about 453 cal, 37 g pro, 26 g total fat (6 g sat. fat), 19 g carb, 3 g fibre, 95 mg chol, 302 mg sodium, 865 mg potassium. % RDI: 15% calcium, 18% iron, 29% vit A, 7% vit C, 25% folate.

Napa Cabbage Slaw With Grilled Chicken

HANDS-ON TIME	TOTAL TIME	MAKES
20 MINUTES	30 MINUTES	4 SERVINGS

What you need

2	boneless skinless chicken breasts (about 450 g total)
pinch	each salt and pepper
4 cups	lightly packed shredded napa cabbage
1	carrot, grated or julienned (see tip, below)
1	sweet red pepper, thinly sliced
1	rib celery, thinly sliced diagonally
half	English cucumber, halved lengthwise, seeded and thinly sliced diagonally
2	green onions, thinly sliced
⅓ cup	sliced almonds, toasted (see tip, page 27)

SOY VINAIGRETTE:

2 tbsp	vegetable oil
4 tsp	unseasoned rice vinegar
1 tbsp	sodium-reduced soy sauce
2 tsp	sesame oil
pinch	salt

How to make it

Sprinkle chicken with salt and pepper. Place on greased grill over medium-high heat; close lid and grill, turning once, until no longer pink inside, 12 to 15 minutes. Let stand for 5 minutes before slicing.

SOY VINAIGRETTE: Meanwhile, in large bowl, whisk together vegetable oil, vinegar, soy sauce, sesame oil and salt.

Add cabbage, carrot, red pepper, celery, cucumber and green onions to vinaigrette; toss to coat. Top with chicken; sprinkle with almonds.

VARIATION

Creamy Tahini Slaw With Grilled Chicken

Replace soy vinaigrette with a mixture of 2 tbsp olive oil, 4 tsp lemon juice, 1 tbsp tahini, 1 tbsp Balkan-style plain yogurt and ¼ tsp each salt and pepper.

TIP FROM THE TEST KITCHEN

Grating is a fast way to cut the carrots for this salad. Julienning them can also be quick if you use a mandoline instead of a knife.

NUTRITIONAL INFORMATION, PER SERVING: about 293 cal, 30 g pro, 15 g total fat (2 g sat. fat), 11 g carb, 3 g fibre, 67 mg chol, 242 mg sodium, 786 mg potassium. % RDI: 10% calcium, 11% iron, 40% vit A, 123% vit C, 39% folate.

Grilled Halloumi and Asparagus Salad

HANDS-ON TIME
15 MINUTES

•

TOTAL TIME
15 MINUTES

•

MAKES
4 SERVINGS

What you need

1	bunch (450 g) asparagus, trimmed (see tip, page 16)
1	pkg (250 g) halloumi cheese, cut in ½-inch (1 cm) thick slices
1	head Boston lettuce, torn
4 cups	torn romaine lettuce
¾ cup	cherry tomatoes, halved
2 tbsp	olive oil
2 tsp	red wine vinegar
pinch	each salt and pepper

How to make it

Place asparagus on greased grill over medium-high heat; close lid and grill, turning often, for 3 minutes.

Add halloumi cheese; grill, covered and turning once, until asparagus is tender and slightly grill-marked, and halloumi is grill-marked, about 4 minutes.

Meanwhile, on platter, combine Boston lettuce, romaine lettuce and cherry tomatoes. Whisk together oil, vinegar, salt and pepper; drizzle over salad. Toss to coat. Top with asparagus and halloumi cheese.

VARIATION

Skillet Halloumi and Asparagus Salad

In large nonstick skillet, heat 2 tsp vegetable oil over medium heat; cook asparagus until tender-crisp, about 10 minutes. Set aside. In same skillet over medium heat, cook halloumi, turning once, until golden, about 4 minutes. Continue with recipe.

NUTRITIONAL INFORMATION, PER SERVING: about 304 cal, 16 g pro, 24 g total fat (11 g sat. fat), 9 g carb, 3 g fibre, 63 mg chol, 769 mg sodium, 458 mg potassium. % RDI: 36% calcium, 13% iron, 86% vit A, 37% vit C, 98% folate.

Salt and Pepper Croûtes

MAKES
ABOUT 60 PIECES

What you need

1	ficelle (or half baguette)
¼ cup	extra-virgin olive oil
1½ tsp	coarse sea salt
½ tsp	coarsely ground pepper

How to make it

Cut ficelle into ¼-inch (5 mm) thick slices (if using baguette, halve lengthwise before slicing); arrange on rimmed baking sheet. Brush with half of the oil; sprinkle with half each of the salt and pepper.

Bake in 350°F (180°C) oven for 15 minutes. Turn and brush with remaining oil; sprinkle with remaining salt and pepper. Bake until golden and crisp, about 10 minutes. Let cool. *(Make-ahead: Store in airtight container for up to 2 weeks.)*

NUTRITIONAL INFORMATION, PER PIECE: about 13 cal, trace pro, 1 g total fat (trace sat. fat), 1 g carb, 0 g fibre, 0 mg chol, 50 mg sodium. % RDI: 1% iron.

Easy Crostini

MAKES
24 PIECES

What you need

1	baguette
2 tbsp	extra-virgin olive oil
1	clove garlic, halved

How to make it

Cut baguette into 24 slices; brush with oil. Broil on rimmed baking sheet until golden, about 4 minutes. Rub with cut sides of garlic. *(Make-ahead: Store in airtight container for up to 2 days.)*

NUTRITIONAL INFORMATION, PER PIECE: about 44 cal, 1 g pro, 1 g total fat (trace sat. fat), 7 g carb, trace fibre, 0 mg chol, 77 mg sodium, 15 mg potassium. % RDI: 3% iron, 7% folate.

Parmesan Croutons

MAKES
ABOUT 2 CUPS

What you need

2 cups	cubed (¼ inch/5 mm) day-old bread
⅓ cup	grated Parmigiano-Reggiano cheese
2 tbsp	extra-virgin olive oil
¼ tsp	crumbled dried thyme
pinch	each salt and cayenne pepper

How to make it

Toss together bread cubes, Parmigiano-Reggiano cheese, oil, thyme, salt and cayenne pepper; spread on rimmed baking sheet.

Bake in 350°F (180°C) oven until golden and crisp, 10 minutes. Let cool. *(Make-ahead: Store in airtight container for up to 5 days.)*

NUTRITIONAL INFORMATION, PER 2 TBSP: about 35 cal, 1 g pro, 2 g total fat (1 g sat. fat), 2 g carb, trace fibre, 2 mg chol, 54 mg sodium. % RDI: 3% calcium, 1% iron, 2% folate.

Ricotta Tartlets and Salad With Tarragon Vinaigrette

HANDS-ON TIME	•	TOTAL TIME	•	MAKES
15 MINUTES		35 MINUTES		6 SERVINGS

What you need

| 8 cups | mixed baby greens |
| ¼ cup | finely chopped fresh chives or green onions |

RICOTTA TARTLETS:

½ cup	grated Parmesan cheese
1 cup	ricotta cheese
1	egg white
1 tbsp	chopped fresh thyme
1 tbsp	all-purpose flour
¼ tsp	pepper
¼ tsp	baking powder
¼ tsp	crumbled dried lavender (optional)

TARRAGON VINAIGRETTE:

1 tbsp	tarragon vinegar or white wine vinegar
1 tsp	Dijon mustard
¼ tsp	crumbled dried savory
pinch	each salt and pepper
¼ cup	extra-virgin olive oil

How to make it

RICOTTA TARTLETS: Grease 12 mini-muffin cups; sprinkle sides and bottoms with 2 tbsp of the Parmesan cheese to coat evenly. Set aside. In bowl, beat together ricotta cheese, egg white, remaining Parmesan cheese, thyme, flour, pepper, baking powder, and lavender (if using) until smooth.

Spoon into prepared mini-muffin cups; smooth tops. Bake in 350°F (180°C) oven until puffed and cake tester inserted in centre of several comes out clean, about 20 minutes. Let cool in pan on rack for 5 minutes.

TARRAGON VINAIGRETTE: In large bowl, whisk together tarragon vinegar, mustard, savory, salt and pepper; slowly whisk in oil until emulsified.

Add baby greens and chives to vinaigrette; toss to coat. Divide among 6 plates; top each with 2 tartlets.

TIP FROM THE TEST KITCHEN
The tartlets in this recipe also make elegant bases for canapés and are delicious floated on creamy soups.

NUTRITIONAL INFORMATION, PER SERVING: about 209 cal, 10 g pro, 17 g total fat (6 g sat. fat), 5 g carb, 1 g fibre, 28 mg chol, 212 mg sodium. % RDI: 22% calcium, 8% iron, 23% vit A, 20% vit C, 32% folate.

Fig, Prosciutto and Gorgonzola Salad

HANDS-ON TIME	•	TOTAL TIME	•	MAKES
10 MINUTES		10 MINUTES		4 SERVINGS

What you need

6	slices prosciutto (115 g)
12	dried Mission figs, halved (or 6 fresh figs, quartered)
12 cups	mixed baby greens (such as arugula, spinach, mâche and/or romaine)
115 g	Gorgonzola cheese, crumbled
¼ cup	sliced almonds, toasted (see tip, page 27)

BALSAMIC DRESSING:

¼ cup	balsamic vinegar
2 tbsp	liquid honey
1 tsp	Dijon mustard
pinch	each salt and pepper
⅓ cup	extra-virgin olive oil

How to make it

BALSAMIC DRESSING: In small bowl, whisk together vinegar, honey, mustard, salt and pepper; slowly whisk in oil until emulsified.

Cut each prosciutto slice lengthwise into 4 strips; wrap each around 1 fig half. Arrange baby greens on serving platter; top with figs, then Gorgonzola cheese. Drizzle with half of the dressing, reserving remainder for another use. (*Make-ahead: Refrigerate dressing in airtight container for up to 5 days.*)

Sprinkle with almonds.

VARIATION

Grilled Fig, Prosciutto and Gorgonzola Salad

Thread wrapped figs onto metal skewers. Place on greased grill over medium-high heat; close lid and grill, turning once, until prosciutto is slightly crisp, about 5 minutes.

NUTRITIONAL INFORMATION, PER SERVING: about 399 cal, 18 g pro, 26 g total fat (9 g sat. fat), 28 g carb, 5 g fibre, 57 mg chol, 1,184 mg sodium, 879 mg potassium. % RDI: 28% calcium, 25% iron, 94% vit A, 55% vit C, 59% folate.

Pork Tostada Salad

HANDS-ON TIME	•	TOTAL TIME	•	MAKES
25 MINUTES		25 MINUTES		4 SERVINGS

What you need

450 g	lean ground pork
1 tbsp	chili powder
1 tbsp	wine vinegar
½ tsp	each salt and ground coriander
pinch	granulated sugar
2	cloves garlic, minced
2	green onions, thinly sliced (light and dark green parts separated)
8	corn tostadas (see tip, below)
2 cups	shredded iceberg or romaine lettuce
1	large tomato, chopped
½ cup	salsa
½ cup	shredded Cheddar cheese
¼ cup	light sour cream

How to make it

In large skillet, cook pork over medium-high heat, breaking up with spoon, until no longer pink, about 5 minutes.

Drain fat from pan; add chili powder, vinegar, salt, coriander, sugar, garlic and light green parts of green onions. Reduce heat to medium; cook, stirring often, for 5 minutes.

Place 1 tostada on each of 4 plates; top with about half each of the lettuce, tomato, pork mixture, salsa and Cheddar cheese. Repeat layers once, starting with tostada. Top with sour cream; sprinkle with dark green parts of green onions.

TIP FROM THE TEST KITCHEN

Tostadas are flat, crunchy taco shells that do not require heating. Look for plain and flavoured varieties in the Mexican section of the grocery store. If you can't find tostadas, use tortilla chips instead.

NUTRITIONAL INFORMATION, PER SERVING: about 422 cal, 28 g pro, 26 g total fat (10 g sat. fat), 21 g carb, 4 g fibre, 93 mg chol, 748 mg sodium. % RDI: 18% calcium, 16% iron, 16% vit A, 18% vit C, 17% folate.

Pork and Napa Salad

HANDS-ON TIME	TOTAL TIME	MAKES
30 MINUTES	45 MINUTES	4 SERVINGS

What you need

1 tbsp	vegetable oil
2	cloves garlic, minced
½ tsp	each salt and pepper
½ tsp	ground coriander
¼ tsp	ground cloves
450 g	pork tenderloin
6 cups	shredded napa cabbage
1	carrot, julienned
1 cup	sugar snap peas, blanched (see tip, below) and halved
2	green onions, thinly sliced
2 tbsp	lime juice
1 tbsp	sesame oil
1 tbsp	vinegar
1 tbsp	fish sauce
2 tsp	granulated sugar
2 tsp	minced fresh ginger

How to make it

Stir together oil, garlic, salt, pepper, coriander and cloves; brush over pork. Let stand for 15 minutes.

Place pork on greased grill over medium-high heat; close lid and grill, turning 3 times, until juices run clear when pork is pierced and just a hint of pink remains inside, or instant-read thermometer inserted in thickest part reads 160°F (71°C), 15 to 20 minutes. Transfer to cutting board and tent with foil; let stand for 5 minutes before cutting into ½-inch (1 cm) thick slices.

Meanwhile, in bowl, combine cabbage, carrot, snap peas, green onions, lime juice, sesame oil, vinegar, fish sauce, sugar and ginger; toss to coat. Divide among 4 plates. Top with pork.

TIP FROM THE TEST KITCHEN
For this salad, the snap peas need only 1 to 2 minutes of blanching in boiling water to be perfectly tender-crisp. Transfer them to a bowl of ice water after cooking and let them cool completely.

NUTRITIONAL INFORMATION, PER SERVING: about 247 cal, 28 g pro, 10 g total fat (2 g sat. fat), 13 g carb, 3 g fibre, 61 mg chol, 715 mg sodium. % RDI: 11% calcium, 16% iron, 31% vit A, 68% vit C, 53% folate.

Pancetta and Egg on Hearty Greens

HANDS-ON TIME	•	TOTAL TIME	•	MAKES
30 MINUTES		30 MINUTES		4 SERVINGS

What you need

How to make it

1 tbsp	extra-virgin olive oil
8	thin slices pancetta
1	pkg (340 g) mixed mushrooms, sliced
pinch	each salt and pepper
1	head frisée, torn
1	head radicchio, torn
4	eggs, poached (see tip, below)

SHALLOT CAPER DRESSING:

⅓ cup	thinly sliced shallots
2 tbsp	white wine vinegar
1 tbsp	drained capers, finely chopped
2 tsp	Dijon mustard
pinch	granulated sugar
pinch	each salt and pepper
⅓ cup	extra-virgin olive oil

SHALLOT CAPER DRESSING: In bowl, stir together shallots, vinegar, capers, mustard, sugar, salt and pepper; slowly whisk in oil until emulsified. Set aside.

In large skillet, heat oil over medium-high heat; cook pancetta until crisp, about 4 minutes. Drain on paper towel–lined plate.

Drain all but 2 tbsp fat from pan; cook mushrooms, salt and pepper over medium heat, stirring occasionally, until tender and golden, about 6 minutes.

In large bowl, toss together frisée, radicchio, mushroom mixture and dressing. Divide among 4 plates; top each with pancetta and egg.

TIP FROM THE TEST KITCHEN

To poach eggs, in a large saucepan, bring 2 to 3 inches (5 to 8 cm) of water to a simmer over medium heat. Add 1 tbsp vinegar. One at a time, crack the eggs into a small bowl; gently slide them into the simmering water. Reduce the heat to low; cook until the whites are set and the yolks are still runny, about 3 minutes. Using a slotted spoon, transfer the eggs to a paper towel–lined tray and blot dry.

NUTRITIONAL INFORMATION, PER SERVING: about 395 cal, 16 g pro, 33 g total fat (6 g sat. fat), 13 g carb, 4 g fibre, 206 mg chol, 498 mg sodium, 976 mg potassium. % RDI: 11% calcium, 22% iron, 35% vit A, 22% vit C, 113% folate.

Grilled Steak and Asparagus Salad

HANDS-ON TIME	TOTAL TIME	MAKES
15 MINUTES	15 MINUTES	4 SERVINGS

What you need

½ tsp	celery seeds
¼ tsp	each salt and pepper
¼ tsp	garlic powder
450 g	beef strip loin grilling steak, about 1 inch (2.5 cm) thick
1	red onion, cut in ½-inch (1 cm) thick rings
2 tsp	olive oil
1	bunch (450 g) asparagus, trimmed (see tip, page 16)
6 cups	torn romaine lettuce hearts
70 g	pepper-crusted goat cheese, crumbled

PESTO VINAIGRETTE:

¼ cup	extra-virgin olive oil
3 tbsp	balsamic vinegar
2 tbsp	sun-dried tomato pesto
¼ tsp	pepper

How to make it

Combine celery seeds, salt, pepper and garlic powder; rub all over steak. Brush onion with some of the oil; toss asparagus with remaining oil.

Place steak, onion and asparagus on greased grill over medium-high heat; close lid and grill, turning once, until steak is medium-rare, onion is softened and asparagus is tender-crisp, about 8 minutes. Transfer to cutting board; let steak stand for 5 minutes before thinly slicing. Meanwhile, halve onion rings and asparagus.

PESTO VINAIGRETTE: Meanwhile, in large bowl, whisk together oil, vinegar, pesto and pepper. Add lettuce, onion and asparagus; toss to coat. Sprinkle with goat cheese; top with steak.

NUTRITIONAL INFORMATION, PER SERVING: about 427 cal, 33 g pro, 26 g total fat (8 g sat. fat), 15 g carb, 4 g fibre, 64 mg chol, 339 mg sodium, 685 mg potassium. % RDI: 8% calcium, 32% iron, 57% vit A, 38% vit C, 92% folate.

Steak Salad With Tangy Blue Cheese Dressing

HANDS-ON TIME	TOTAL TIME	MAKES
15 MINUTES	30 MINUTES	4 SERVINGS

What you need

450 g	beef strip loin grilling steak, about 1 inch (2.5 cm) thick
½ tsp	each salt and pepper
1	head Boston or Bibb lettuce, torn
½ cup	thinly sliced radishes
½ cup	cherry tomatoes, halved
1	avocado, pitted, peeled and sliced
2	green onions, chopped

TANGY BLUE CHEESE DRESSING:

⅓ cup	buttermilk
¼ cup	crumbled blue cheese
3 tbsp	light mayonnaise
1 tsp	white wine vinegar
1 tsp	Dijon mustard

How to make it

TANGY BLUE CHEESE DRESSING: In food processor, purée together buttermilk, blue cheese, mayonnaise, vinegar and mustard until smooth. Set aside.

Sprinkle steak with salt and pepper. Place on greased grill or in grill pan over medium-high heat; close lid and grill, turning once, until medium-rare, about 8 minutes. Transfer to cutting board and tent with foil; let stand for 10 minutes before thinly slicing across the grain.

Meanwhile, divide lettuce, radishes, tomatoes and avocado among 4 plates. Top with steak and blue cheese dressing; sprinkle with green onions.

NUTRITIONAL INFORMATION, PER SERVING: about 369 cal, 26 g pro, 27 g total fat (9 g sat. fat), 9 g carb, 5 g fibre, 72 mg chol, 576 mg sodium, 795 mg potassium. % RDI: 11% calcium, 18% iron, 9% vit A, 26% vit C, 42% folate.

Creamy Feta-Yogurt Dressing

MAKES
ABOUT ⅔ CUP

What you need

½ cup	crumbled feta cheese
1	small clove garlic, grated or pressed
¼ cup	2% plain Greek yogurt
1 tbsp	extra-virgin olive oil
1 tbsp	lemon juice
1 tsp	liquid honey
pinch	pepper

How to make it

In bowl and using fork, mash feta cheese with garlic until in coarse crumbs. Stir in yogurt, oil, lemon juice, honey and pepper.

NUTRITIONAL INFORMATION, PER 1 TBSP: about 36 cal, 2 g pro, 3 g total fat (1 g sat. fat), 1 g carb, 0 g fibre, 7 mg chol, 82 mg sodium. % RDI: 4% calcium, 1% iron, 1% vit A, 1% folate.

Thousand Island Dressing

MAKES
ABOUT 1½ CUPS

What you need

1 cup	light mayonnaise
2 tbsp	finely chopped sweet pickles
2 tbsp	each finely chopped drained capers and green olives
2 tbsp	ketchup or tomato-based chili sauce
2 tbsp	water
1 tbsp	cider vinegar
pinch	pepper

How to make it

In small bowl, whisk together mayonnaise, pickles, capers, green olives, ketchup, water, vinegar and pepper. *(Make-ahead: Refrigerate in airtight container for up to 1 week.)*

NUTRITIONAL INFORMATION, PER 1 TBSP: about 36 cal, trace pro, 3 g total fat (1 g sat. fat), 2 g carb, 0 g fibre, 3 mg chol, 121 mg sodium. % RDI: 1% iron, 1% vit A.

Creamy Dill Ranch Dressing

MAKES
1⅓ CUPS

What you need

⅔ cup	buttermilk
⅓ cup	light mayonnaise
2 tsp	cider vinegar
½ tsp	Dijon mustard
¼ tsp	pepper
pinch	salt
dash	hot pepper sauce
1 tbsp	each chopped fresh dill and parsley

How to make it

In liquid measure or small bowl, whisk together buttermilk, mayonnaise, vinegar, mustard, pepper, salt and hot pepper sauce. Stir in dill and parsley. *(Make-ahead: Refrigerate in airtight container for up to 3 days.)*

NUTRITIONAL INFORMATION, PER 1 TBSP: about 17 cal, trace pro, 1 g total fat (trace sat. fat), 1 g carb, 0 g fibre, 2 mg chol, 33 mg sodium. % RDI: 1% calcium.

Grilled Steak and Potato Salad

HANDS-ON TIME	TOTAL TIME	MAKES
25 MINUTES	30 MINUTES	4 SERVINGS

What you need

2 tbsp	olive oil
1 tsp	each sweet paprika and dried oregano
¼ tsp	each salt and pepper
450 g	mini red-skinned potatoes (about 16)
450 g	beef flank marinating steak
8 cups	lightly packed mixed baby greens
1 cup	thinly sliced cored fennel bulb
1 cup	halved grape tomatoes
¼ cup	crumbled blue cheese

EASY DIJON VINAIGRETTE:

2 tbsp	extra-virgin olive oil
1 tbsp	wine vinegar
1 tsp	Dijon mustard
pinch	each salt and pepper

How to make it

Stir together oil, paprika, oregano, salt and pepper; set aside.

Scrub and halve potatoes. Place in microwaveable dish; sprinkle with 2 tbsp water. Cover and microwave on high until tender, 5 to 8 minutes. Toss with half of the paprika mixture; thread onto metal or soaked wooden skewers.

Rub remaining paprika mixture all over steak. Place steak and potatoes on greased grill over medium-high heat; close lid and grill, turning once, until steak is medium-rare and potatoes are tender, 10 to 12 minutes.

Transfer steak to cutting board; let stand for 5 minutes before thinly slicing across the grain. Remove potatoes from skewers.

EASY DIJON VINAIGRETTE: Meanwhile, in large bowl, whisk together oil, vinegar, mustard, salt and pepper.

Add baby greens, fennel, tomatoes, potatoes and steak to vinaigrette; toss to coat. Sprinkle with blue cheese.

NUTRITIONAL INFORMATION, PER SERVING: about 428 cal, 30 g pro, 23 g total fat (6 g sat. fat), 25 g carb, 5 g fibre, 55 mg chol, 366 mg sodium, 1,231 mg potassium. % RDI: 14% calcium, 31% iron, 31% vit A, 67% vit C, 58% folate.

Curried Lentil, Wild Rice and Orzo Salad

HANDS-ON TIME	•	TOTAL TIME	•	MAKES
10 MINUTES		4¾ HOURS		12 SERVINGS

What you need

½ cup	wild rice
⅔ cup	dried green or brown lentils (see tip, below)
½ cup	orzo pasta
½ cup	dried currants
¼ cup	finely chopped red onion
⅓ cup	slivered almonds, toasted (see tip, page 27)

CURRY DRESSING:

¼ cup	white wine vinegar
1 tsp	ground cumin
1 tsp	Dijon mustard
½ tsp	each granulated sugar and salt
½ tsp	ground coriander
¼ tsp	each turmeric, sweet paprika and nutmeg
pinch	each cinnamon, ground cloves and cayenne pepper
⅓ cup	canola or vegetable oil

How to make it

In large pot of boiling salted water, cover and cook wild rice for 10 minutes.

Add lentils; cook for 20 minutes. Add orzo; cook just until tender, about 5 minutes. Drain well; transfer to large bowl. Add currants and red onion.

CURRY DRESSING: In small bowl, whisk together vinegar, cumin, mustard, sugar, salt, coriander, turmeric, paprika, nutmeg, cinnamon, cloves and cayenne pepper; whisk in oil.

Pour dressing over wild rice mixture; gently toss to coat. Let cool. Cover and refrigerate until chilled, about 4 hours. *(Make-ahead: Refrigerate for up to 24 hours.)*

Serve sprinkled with almonds.

TIP FROM THE TEST KITCHEN
Dried lentils are convenient because they don't require soaking. Red lentils are small, mild and good in stews, soups and dips, but won't hold their shape in salads. Brown lentils are sturdier, with a spicy taste that works well in salads, soups and stews. Richly flavoured green lentils become firm yet tender when cooked, making them ideal in salads.

NUTRITIONAL INFORMATION, PER SERVING: about 178 cal, 6 g pro, 8 g total fat (1 g sat. fat), 22 g carb, 3 g fibre, 0 mg chol, 178 mg sodium, 231 mg potassium. % RDI: 2% calcium, 13% iron, 2% vit C, 30% folate.

Gluten-Free Quinoa Salad With Creamy Tahini Dressing

HANDS-ON TIME	•	TOTAL TIME	•	MAKES
30 MINUTES		45 MINUTES		4 TO 6 SERVINGS

What you need

1 cup	quinoa, rinsed and drained (see tip, below)
¼ tsp	salt
2 cups	grape or cherry tomatoes, halved
1 cup	diced English cucumber
1 cup	rinsed drained canned lentils
⅔ cup	chopped fresh parsley
⅓ cup	chopped fresh mint
3	green onions, thinly sliced

CREAMY TAHINI DRESSING:

¼ cup	lemon juice
¼ cup	extra-virgin olive oil
¼ cup	warm water
¼ cup	tahini
1	small clove garlic, minced
½ tsp	ground cumin
¼ tsp	pepper
¼ tsp	salt

How to make it

In saucepan, bring 2 cups water, quinoa and salt to boil over high heat; reduce heat, cover and simmer until no liquid remains and quinoa is tender, about 15 minutes. Let cool.

CREAMY TAHINI DRESSING: In large bowl, whisk together lemon juice, oil, warm water, tahini, garlic, cumin, pepper and salt.

Add quinoa, tomatoes, cucumber, lentils, parsley, mint and green onions to dressing; toss to coat. *(Make-ahead: Cover and refrigerate for up to 3 days.)*

TIP FROM THE TEST KITCHEN
Quinoa is naturally coated with a bitter protective compound called saponin. Most quinoa is labelled "ready to use," but we recommend rinsing it thoroughly under cold running water to be sure any traces of bitterness are gone. Drain the quinoa well before proceeding with the recipe.

NUTRITIONAL INFORMATION, PER EACH OF 6 SERVINGS:
about 300 cal, 9 g pro, 16 g total fat (2 g sat. fat), 32 g carb, 6 g fibre, 0 mg chol, 291 mg sodium, 581 mg potassium. % RDI: 9% calcium, 43% iron, 12% vit A, 33% vit C, 48% folate.

Quinoa and Chickpea Salad With Tomato Vinaigrette

HANDS-ON TIME	TOTAL TIME	MAKES
20 MINUTES	35 MINUTES	4 SERVINGS

What you need

1 cup	quinoa, rinsed and drained (see tip, page 67)
2 cups	green beans, trimmed and chopped
1	can (540 mL) chickpeas, drained and rinsed
1	sweet red pepper, diced
1 cup	crumbled feta cheese

TOMATO VINAIGRETTE:

⅓ cup	bottled strained tomatoes (passata)
3 tbsp	red wine vinegar
3 tbsp	olive oil
3 tbsp	liquid honey
½ tsp	dried Italian herb seasoning
½ tsp	salt
¼ tsp	pepper
pinch	cayenne pepper

How to make it

In saucepan, bring quinoa and 2 cups water to boil; reduce heat, cover and simmer for 12 minutes. Fluff with fork; let cool.

Meanwhile, in saucepan of boiling salted water, blanch green beans until tender-crisp, about 3 minutes. Using tongs, transfer to bowl of ice water; let cool. Drain well; transfer to large bowl. Stir in cooled quinoa, chickpeas, red pepper and feta cheese.

TOMATO VINAIGRETTE: Whisk together strained tomatoes, vinegar, oil, honey, Italian herb seasoning, salt, pepper and cayenne pepper; pour over quinoa mixture. Stir to coat.

NUTRITIONAL INFORMATION, PER SERVING: about 556 cal, 18 g pro, 22 g total fat (8 g sat. fat), 75 g carb, 9 g fibre, 35 mg chol, 1,155 mg sodium, 649 mg potassium. % RDI: 25% calcium, 46% iron, 18% vit A, 108% vit C, 53% folate.

Marinated Chickpea Salad

HANDS-ON TIME	•	TOTAL TIME	•	MAKES
10 MINUTES		2¼ HOURS		4 SERVINGS

What you need

3 tbsp	lemon juice
2 tbsp	olive oil
¾ tsp	ground coriander
¼ tsp	pepper
pinch	cayenne pepper
pinch	salt
1	can (540 mL) chickpeas, drained and rinsed
1	baby cucumber, quartered lengthwise and sliced
⅓ cup	diced red onion
¼ cup	chopped fresh cilantro

How to make it

In bowl, whisk together lemon juice, oil, coriander, pepper, cayenne pepper and salt.

Add chickpeas, cucumber and red onion; stir to combine. Cover and refrigerate for 2 hours. *(Make-ahead: Refrigerate for up to 24 hours.)*

Stir in chopped cilantro.

TIP FROM THE TEST KITCHEN
Cilantro is often gritty, so it requires a good rinse before you use it in recipes. Wash and store it the same way you do salad greens (see page 8 for how-tos).

NUTRITIONAL INFORMATION, PER SERVING: about 199 cal, 6 g pro, 8 g total fat (1 g sat. fat), 27 g carb, 5 g fibre, 0 mg chol, 279 mg sodium, 226 mg potassium. % RDI: 4% calcium, 11% iron, 1% vit A, 17% vit C, 31% folate.

Honey-Lime Oat and Black Bean Salad

HANDS-ON TIME	•	TOTAL TIME	•	MAKES
15 MINUTES		2 HOURS		6 SERVINGS

What you need

1 cup	oat groats
1 cup	rinsed drained canned black beans
1 cup	halved cherry tomatoes
1	jalapeño pepper, seeded and finely chopped
2 tbsp	finely chopped red onion
half	ripe avocado, pitted, peeled and diced
1 tbsp	chopped fresh cilantro

HONEY-LIME VINAIGRETTE:

3 tbsp	vegetable oil
1 tsp	grated lime zest
3 tbsp	lime juice
1 tbsp	liquid honey
¼ tsp	chili powder
¼ tsp	each salt and pepper

How to make it

In large saucepan, bring 2 cups water to boil; add oat groats. Reduce heat and simmer, uncovered and stirring occasionally, until tender and no liquid remains, about 45 minutes. Drain and rinse under cold water; drain.

HONEY-LIME VINAIGRETTE: Meanwhile, whisk together oil, lime zest, lime juice, honey, chili powder, salt and pepper.

In large bowl, combine oat groats, beans, tomatoes, jalapeño pepper and red onion. Add vinaigrette; toss to coat. Cover and refrigerate for 1 hour. *(Make-ahead: Refrigerate in airtight container for up to 24 hours.)*

Just before serving, stir in avocado; sprinkle with cilantro.

VARIATION

Honey-Lime Whole Grain and Black Bean Salad

Substitute any whole grain, such as wheat berries, whole spelt or brown rice, for the oat groats, cooking according to package directions.

NUTRITIONAL INFORMATION, PER SERVING: about 241 cal, 7 g pro, 11 g total fat (1 g sat. fat), 30 g carb, 6 g fibre, 0 mg chol, 205 mg sodium, 368 mg potassium. % RDI: 3% calcium, 14% iron, 3% vit A, 17% vit C, 17% folate.

Wheat Berry, Corn and Red Pepper Salad

HANDS-ON TIME	•	TOTAL TIME	•	MAKES
10 MINUTES		2¼ HOURS		8 SERVINGS

What you need

1 cup	wheat berries
1 cup	frozen corn kernels
1	sweet red pepper, diced
4	green onions, sliced
5	leaves fresh basil, cut in thin strips

SMOKED PAPRIKA VINAIGRETTE:

3 tbsp	white wine vinegar
1	clove garlic, minced
1 tsp	Dijon mustard
½ tsp	smoked paprika
¼ tsp	each salt and pepper
3 tbsp	vegetable oil

How to make it

SMOKED PAPRIKA VINAIGRETTE: In large bowl, whisk together vinegar, garlic, mustard, paprika, salt and pepper; slowly whisk in oil until emulsified. Set aside.

In saucepan of boiling salted water, cook wheat berries until tender, about 1 hour. Add corn; cook for 30 seconds. Drain and rinse under cold water; drain again. Add to bowl with vinaigrette.

Add red pepper, green onions and basil; toss to combine. Cover and refrigerate for 1 hour before serving. (*Make-ahead: Refrigerate in airtight container for up to 24 hours.*)

NUTRITIONAL INFORMATION, PER SERVING: about 149 cal, 4 g pro, 6 g total fat (1 g sat. fat), 23 g carb, 4 g fibre, 0 mg chol, 506 mg sodium, 188 mg potassium. % RDI: 2% calcium, 8% iron, 7% vit A, 43% vit C, 9% folate.

Lentil and Sweet Potato Salad

HANDS-ON TIME	•	TOTAL TIME	•	MAKES
10 MINUTES		35 MINUTES		2 SERVINGS

What you need | How to make it

½ cup	dried green lentils (see tip, page 66)
1	sweet potato, peeled and cubed
3 tbsp	extra-virgin olive oil
2 tbsp	balsamic vinegar
¼ tsp	each salt and pepper
1 cup	baby arugula
¼ cup	crumbled soft goat cheese

In large saucepan of boiling water, cook lentils until tender, about 25 minutes. Drain.

Meanwhile, toss sweet potato with 1 tsp of the oil. Roast on baking sheet in 400°F (200°C) oven, turning once, until golden and tender, about 15 minutes.

In bowl, whisk together balsamic vinegar, remaining oil, salt and pepper; add lentils, sweet potato and arugula. Toss to coat; top with goat cheese.

TIP FROM THE TEST KITCHEN

This recipe doubles easily if you need to feed more people. Another night, make a double batch of only the roasted sweet potato and serve it as a healthier alternative to sweet potato fries.

NUTRITIONAL INFORMATION, PER SERVING: about 554 cal, 19 g pro, 25 g total fat (5 g sat. fat), 67 g carb, 11 g fibre, 8 mg chol, 413 mg sodium, 1,032 mg potassium. % RDI: 11% calcium, 49% iron, 319% vit A, 48% vit C, 125% folate.

Green Bean and Barley Salad

HANDS-ON TIME	•	TOTAL TIME	•	MAKES
10 MINUTES		40 MINUTES		12 SERVINGS

What you need

450 g	green beans
1 cup	pot barley or pearl barley
¼ cup	extra-virgin olive oil
3 tbsp	white wine vinegar
1	clove garlic, minced
1½ tsp	minced fresh thyme
1½ tsp	Dijon mustard
½ tsp	salt
¼ tsp	pepper
4 cups	baby arugula
2 cups	grape or cherry tomatoes, halved
2	green onions, thinly sliced
⅔ cup	crumbled feta cheese (about 100 g)

How to make it

Trim green beans; halve diagonally. In saucepan of boiling water, blanch green beans until tender-crisp, about 3 minutes. Using tongs, transfer to bowl of ice water; let cool. Drain well; pat dry.

Meanwhile, in pot of boiling salted water, cook barley until tender, 20 to 25 minutes. Drain; let cool for 5 minutes.

In large bowl, whisk together oil, vinegar, garlic, thyme, mustard, salt and pepper; add barley and green beans. Toss to coat.

Add arugula, tomatoes and green onions; toss well. *(Make-ahead: Cover and let stand for up to 1 hour or refrigerate for up to 4 hours.)* Stir in feta cheese.

NUTRITIONAL INFORMATION, PER SERVING: about 142 cal, 4 g pro, 7 g total fat (2 g sat. fat), 18 g carb, 3 g fibre, 8 mg chol, 254 mg sodium, 231 mg potassium. % RDI: 9% calcium, 9% iron, 10% vit A, 17% vit C, 20% folate.

Three-Bean Salad

HANDS-ON TIME	•	TOTAL TIME	•	MAKES
15 MINUTES		25 MINUTES		6 TO 8 SERVINGS

What you need

1½ cups	cut (2 inches/5 cm) green and/or yellow beans (see tip, below)
¼ cup	extra-virgin olive oil
¼ cup	wine vinegar
1	clove garlic, minced
2 tbsp	chopped fresh parsley
½ tsp	granulated sugar
½ tsp	salt
¼ tsp	dried oregano
¼ tsp	pepper
1	can (540 mL) chickpeas, drained and rinsed
1	can (540 mL) red kidney beans, drained and rinsed
2	green onions, thinly sliced

How to make it

In saucepan of boiling salted water, blanch green beans until tender-crisp, 3 to 5 minutes. Using tongs, transfer to bowl of ice water; let cool. Drain well; shake off water. Place on tea towel; pat dry. Set aside.

In large bowl, whisk together oil, vinegar, garlic, parsley, sugar, salt, oregano and pepper.

Add chickpeas, kidney beans, green onions and green beans; toss to coat. (*Make-ahead: Cover and refrigerate for up to 8 hours.*)

TIP FROM THE TEST KITCHEN
Freshly picked yellow beans are especially delicious in this recipe. Look for them at farmer's markets between July and September, when they're at their peak.

NUTRITIONAL INFORMATION, PER EACH OF 8 SERVINGS:
about 197 cal, 7 g pro, 8 g total fat (1 g sat. fat), 26 g carb, 8 g fibre, 0 mg chol, 505 mg sodium. % RDI: 4% calcium, 13% iron, 2% vit A, 10% vit C, 33% folate.

Tabbouleh

HANDS-ON TIME	TOTAL TIME	MAKES
20 MINUTES	40 MINUTES	4 SERVINGS

What you need

½ cup	medium bulgur (see tip, below)
3 cups	chopped seeded tomatoes
1 cup	minced fresh parsley
¼ cup	minced fresh mint
4	green onions, minced
½ cup	lemon juice
¼ cup	extra-virgin olive oil
¼ tsp	each salt and pepper

How to make it

Place bulgur in fine-mesh sieve; rinse several times with water. Transfer to bowl; cover with ½ inch (1 cm) water. Let stand for 20 minutes. Drain; 1 handful at a time, squeeze out excess water.

In large bowl, combine bulgur, tomatoes, parsley, mint and green onions. Whisk together lemon juice, oil, salt and pepper; add to bulgur mixture. Toss to coat. *(Make-ahead: Cover and set aside for up to 8 hours.)*

TIP FROM THE TEST KITCHEN

Bulgur is ground to different coarseness levels. Medium bulgur is an all-purpose grind that's just right for tabbouleh.

NUTRITIONAL INFORMATION, PER SERVING: about 223 cal, 4 g pro, 14 g total fat (2 g sat. fat), 23 g carb, 6 g fibre, 0 mg chol, 178 mg sodium. % RDI: 6% calcium, 20% iron, 28% vit A, 82% vit C, 30% folate.

Mediterranean Barley Rice Salad

HANDS-ON TIME	•	TOTAL TIME	•	MAKES
30 MINUTES		1¼ HOURS		12 TO 16 SERVINGS

What you need

1 cup	pearl barley, rinsed and drained (see tip, below)
1 cup	basmati rice, rinsed and drained
3 cups	cherry tomatoes
half	large red onion
1	sweet red pepper
1	English cucumber
4 cups	baby spinach, coarsely chopped
1	pkg (200 g) feta cheese, crumbled

DRESSING:

½ cup	extra-virgin olive oil
½ cup	lemon juice
1 tsp	dried oregano
1 tsp	salt
½ tsp	pepper

How to make it

In saucepan of boiling salted water, cook barley until tender, about 20 minutes. Drain and rinse under cold water; drain well. Let stand for 10 minutes to dry. Transfer to large bowl.

Meanwhile, in separate saucepan, bring 1½ cups salted water to boil. Add rice; cover, reduce heat and simmer until tender and no liquid remains, about 15 minutes. Let stand for 5 minutes. Add to barley mixture; let cool.

Cut tomatoes in half; add to barley mixture. Cut onion, red pepper and cucumber into 1-inch (2.5 cm) chunks; add to barley mixture. Toss to combine.

DRESSING: Whisk together oil, lemon juice, oregano, salt and pepper; pour over salad. Toss to coat. Refrigerate for 30 minutes. *(Make-ahead: Refrigerate for up to 24 hours.)*

Just before serving, stir in spinach and feta cheese.

TIP FROM THE TEST KITCHEN
Rinsing the barley and rice before cooking will help the grains stay fluffy (not sticky).

NUTRITIONAL INFORMATION, PER EACH OF 16 SERVINGS:
about 197 cal, 4 g pro, 10 g total fat (3 g sat. fat), 24 g carb, 2 g fibre, 12 mg chol, 554 mg sodium, 234 mg potassium. % RDI: 8% calcium, 8% iron, 14% vit A, 38% vit C, 16% folate.

Bean, Mushroom and Wilted Spinach Salad

HANDS-ON TIME	•	TOTAL TIME	•	MAKES
25 MINUTES		25 MINUTES		4 SERVINGS

What you need

225 g	yellow or green beans (see tip, page 79)
1	pkg (170 g) baby spinach
3 tbsp	extra-virgin olive oil
1	small sweet onion, thinly sliced
225 g	cremini mushrooms
1	clove garlic, minced
¼ tsp	each salt and pepper
¼ tsp	dried thyme
1 cup	rinsed drained canned chickpeas
3 tbsp	white wine vinegar
4	hard-cooked eggs (see tip, page 19), quartered
3 tbsp	shaved Asiago cheese

How to make it

In saucepan of boiling water, cook yellow beans until tender-crisp, about 2 minutes. Drain; set aside.

Meanwhile, place spinach in large bowl; set aside.

In large skillet, heat oil over medium-high heat; sauté onion until tender, about 5 minutes. Add mushrooms, garlic, salt, pepper and thyme; cook, stirring occasionally, until mushrooms are tender and golden, about 7 minutes.

Add yellow beans, chickpeas and vinegar; cook until heated through. Add to spinach, tossing to wilt and coat. Arrange salad on plates. Top with eggs; sprinkle with Asiago cheese.

NUTRITIONAL INFORMATION, PER SERVING: about 352 cal, 18 g pro, 18 g total fat (4 g sat. fat), 32 g carb, 10 g fibre, 190 mg chol, 530 mg sodium, 814 mg potassium. % RDI: 18% calcium, 31% iron, 51% vit A, 15% vit C, 76% folate.

Warm Cannellini Bean and Dandelion Salad

HANDS-ON TIME	•	TOTAL TIME	•	MAKES
20 MINUTES		35 MINUTES		8 SERVINGS

What you need

1	bunch (about 280 g) dandelion greens, trimmed (see tip, below)
¼ cup	extra-virgin olive oil
1	onion, chopped
6	cloves garlic, smashed
3	slices prosciutto, thinly sliced crosswise
5	sprigs fresh oregano
¼ tsp	hot pepper flakes
⅓ cup	white wine
1	can (540 mL) cannellini or white kidney beans, drained and rinsed
8 cups	lightly packed baby spinach
4 tsp	balsamic vinegar

How to make it

Cut dandelion greens in half crosswise; set aside. In Dutch oven, heat oil over medium heat; cook onion and garlic, stirring occasionally, until golden, about 5 minutes.

Add prosciutto, oregano and hot pepper flakes; cook, stirring occasionally, until prosciutto is crisp, about 4 minutes.

Add dandelion greens; cook, stirring, for 2 minutes. Stir in wine and beans; cover and cook until greens are softened, about 5 minutes. Discard oregano. Let cool for 3 minutes.

In large bowl, toss together baby spinach, balsamic vinegar and dandelion mixture. Serve warm.

VARIATION
Warm Fava Bean and Dandelion Salad
Substitute fava beans for the cannellini beans.

TIP FROM THE TEST KITCHEN
To prepare the greens, trim off and discard the root ends, and then rinse the leaves well under cold running water. Spin the leaves dry before using or wrap them in a towel and shake to remove excess water.

NUTRITIONAL INFORMATION, PER SERVING: about 159 cal, 7 g pro, 8 g total fat (1 g sat. fat), 15 g carb, 6 g fibre, 6 mg chol, 332 mg sodium, 499 mg potassium. % RDI: 11% calcium, 19% iron, 73% vit A, 35% vit C, 39% folate.

Black Bean and Corn Salad With Monterey Jack Cheese

HANDS-ON TIME		TOTAL TIME		MAKES
10 MINUTES	•	10 MINUTES	•	4 SERVINGS

What you need

2 tbsp	lime juice
2 tbsp	olive oil
1 tbsp	liquid honey
1	clove garlic, minced
1 tsp	chili powder
1	can (540 mL) black beans, drained and rinsed
1 cup	frozen corn kernels, cooked and cooled
½ cup	diced red onion
½ cup	cubed Monterey Jack cheese (see tip, below)
2 tbsp	chopped fresh cilantro

How to make it

In bowl, whisk together lime juice, oil, honey, garlic and chili powder until blended.

Add black beans, corn, onion, Monterey Jack cheese and cilantro; toss to coat.

TIP FROM THE TEST KITCHEN

If you'd like a spicier salad, substitute jalapeño-laced Jack cheese for the plain Monterey Jack.

NUTRITIONAL INFORMATION, PER SERVING: about 282 cal, 12 g pro, 13 g total fat (4 g sat. fat), 33 g carb, 9 g fibre, 15 mg chol, 454 mg sodium, 438 mg potassium. % RDI: 15% calcium, 16% iron, 7% vit A, 15% vit C, 36% folate.

Dill and Feta Quinoa Salad

HANDS-ON TIME	•	**TOTAL TIME**	•	**MAKES**
15 MINUTES		40 MINUTES		4 SERVINGS

What you need

⅔ cup	quinoa, rinsed and drained (see tip, page 67)
¼ cup	olive oil
2 tbsp	red wine vinegar
¼ tsp	each salt and pepper
2	carrots, shredded
2	zucchini, shredded
½ cup	chopped fresh dill (see tip, below)
½ cup	crumbled feta cheese

How to make it

In saucepan, bring 1⅓ cups water and quinoa to boil; reduce heat, cover and simmer for 12 minutes. Fluff with fork; let cool.

In large bowl, whisk together oil, vinegar, salt and pepper.

Add cooled quinoa, carrots, zucchini, dill and feta cheese; toss until well combined.

TIP FROM THE TEST KITCHEN
The flavour of this salad depends on the fresh dill. Don't be tempted to substitute a smaller amount of dried dillweed for this key component.

NUTRITIONAL INFORMATION, PER SERVING: about 281 cal, 7 g pro, 19 g total fat (5 g sat. fat), 22 g carb, 4 g fibre, 17 mg chol, 250 mg sodium, 510 mg potassium. % RDI: 12% calcium, 13% iron, 65% vit A, 33% vit C, 32% folate.

Summertime Barley Salad

HANDS-ON TIME	•	TOTAL TIME	•	MAKES
15 MINUTES		4½ HOURS		6 TO 8 SERVINGS

What you need

1¾ cups	pearl barley, rinsed and drained
1	clove garlic, minced
¼ cup	cider vinegar
2 tbsp	lemon juice
4 tsp	Dijon mustard
¾ tsp	salt
¼ tsp	pepper
¼ cup	extra-virgin olive oil
1 cup	diced medium or aged Gouda cheese
½ cup	diced dried apricots
⅓ cup	salted roasted pepitas (see tip, page 124)

How to make it

In large pot of boiling lightly salted water, cook barley according to package directions. Drain and rinse under cold water; drain well.

In large bowl, stir together garlic, vinegar, lemon juice, mustard, salt and pepper; slowly whisk in oil until emulsified. Add barley, Gouda cheese and apricots; toss to coat. Cover and refrigerate for 4 hours. (*Make-ahead: Refrigerate for up to 24 hours.*)

To serve, toss salad with pepitas.

TIP FROM THE TEST KITCHEN
To give this salad an extra pop of freshness, gently stir in ¼ cup chopped fresh parsley just before serving.

NUTRITIONAL INFORMATION, PER EACH OF 8 SERVINGS:
about 351 cal, 10 g pro, 17 g total fat (5 g sat. fat), 43 g carb, 4 g fibre, 19 mg chol, 887 mg sodium, 322 mg potassium. % RDI: 13% calcium, 21% iron, 6% vit A, 2% vit C, 14% folate.

From top:
Fully Loaded Potato Salad
page 115

Mediterranean Orzo Salad
page 96

Summertime Barley Salad
opposite

Quinoa and Celeriac Salad

HANDS-ON TIME	•	TOTAL TIME	•	MAKES
25 MINUTES		2 HOURS		6 SERVINGS

What you need

1 cup	quinoa, rinsed and drained (see tip, page 67)
½ tsp	each salt and pepper
2 cups	grape tomatoes, halved
1 tbsp	olive oil
2 tsp	balsamic vinegar
⅓ cup	sunflower seeds
1	celeriac (about 565 g)
¼ cup	lemon juice
¼ cup	light mayonnaise
1 tbsp	Dijon mustard
quarter	red onion, thinly sliced
¼ cup	chopped fresh dill

How to make it

In saucepan, bring 2 cups water to boil; add quinoa and ¼ tsp each of the salt and pepper. Reduce heat to medium-low; cover and simmer until tender and no liquid remains, about 12 minutes. Remove from heat; let stand for 15 minutes. Fluff with fork; let cool to room temperature.

Meanwhile, toss together tomatoes, 2 tsp of the oil, vinegar and a pinch each of the remaining salt and pepper. Roast, cut side up, on parchment paper–lined rimmed baking sheet in 375°F (190°C) oven until lightly browned and shrivelled, about 25 minutes. Let cool to room temperature.

Meanwhile, on separate rimmed baking sheet, spread sunflower seeds; add to oven and toast just until golden and fragrant, 5 minutes. Let cool to room temperature.

Meanwhile, trim and peel celeriac. Using mandoline or sharp knife, julienne. Place in large bowl; add lemon juice and remaining oil, salt and pepper. Toss well to coat. Stir in mayonnaise and mustard until blended.

Add cooled quinoa, red onion, half of the sunflower seeds and the dill; mix well. Garnish with remaining sunflower seeds and roasted tomatoes.

TIP FROM THE TEST KITCHEN
Celeriac browns quickly, so toss it with the dressing right after cutting to maintain its creamy colour.

NUTRITIONAL INFORMATION, PER SERVING: about 249 cal, 7 g pro, 12 g total fat (2 g sat. fat), 32 g carb, 5 g fibre, 3 mg chol, 371 mg sodium, 617 mg potassium. % RDI: 6% calcium, 29% iron, 5% vit A, 25% vit C, 21% folate.

Edamame, Red Pepper and Corn Salad

HANDS-ON TIME	TOTAL TIME	MAKES
5 MINUTES	5 MINUTES	4 SERVINGS

What you need

2 tsp	sodium-reduced soy sauce
1 tsp	sesame oil
1 tsp	liquid honey
1	clove garlic, minced
1 cup	frozen shelled edamame (see tip, below), thawed and drained
1 cup	diced sweet red pepper
½ cup	fresh or frozen corn kernels, cooked and cooled

How to make it

In large bowl, whisk together soy sauce, sesame oil, honey and garlic until well blended.

Add edamame, red pepper and corn kernels; toss to coat.

TIP FROM THE TEST KITCHEN

Using shelled edamame—Japanese green soybeans—makes this dish a speedy weeknight option. Look for bags of shelled edamame in the frozen vegetable section of the supermarket.

NUTRITIONAL INFORMATION, PER SERVING: about 78 cal, 4 g pro, 3 g total fat (trace sat. fat), 11 g carb, 2 g fibre, 0 mg chol, 92 mg sodium, 272 mg potassium. % RDI: 2% calcium, 6% iron, 12% vit A, 125% vit C, 47% folate.

Super Summer Whole Grain Salad

HANDS-ON TIME	•	TOTAL TIME	•	MAKES
25 MINUTES		25 MINUTES		4 SERVINGS

What you need

1 cup	precooked five-grain blend (see tip, below)
1	carrot, diced
1	sweet yellow pepper, diced
1	small zucchini, diced
3	radishes, halved and thinly sliced
4 cups	lightly packed baby arugula
¾ cup	cooled cooked peas
⅓ cup	pepitas (see tip, page 124), toasted

CHIVE CITRUS VINAIGRETTE:

3 tbsp	orange juice
2 tbsp	olive oil
1 tbsp	white wine vinegar
¼ tsp	each salt and pepper
¼ cup	chopped fresh chives

How to make it

In saucepan, bring 4 cups water to boil; stir in grain blend. Cook over medium-high heat until tender, 10 to 12 minutes. Drain and transfer to large bowl; let cool.

Add carrot, yellow pepper, zucchini, radishes, arugula and peas to grain blend.

CHIVE CITRUS VINAIGRETTE: Meanwhile, in bowl, whisk together orange juice, oil, vinegar, salt and pepper; stir in chives.

Drizzle vinaigrette over salad; toss to coat. Sprinkle with pepitas.

VARIATION

Super Summer Gluten-Free Whole Grain Salad

Replace five-grain blend with ¾ cup quinoa or brown rice, cooking according to package directions.

TIP FROM THE TEST KITCHEN
Look for precooked grain and legume blends in the grocery store near the rice.

NUTRITIONAL INFORMATION, PER SERVING: about 324 cal, 11 g pro, 13 g total fat (2 g sat. fat), 23 g carb, 6 g fibre, 0 mg chol, 187 mg sodium, 440 mg potassium. % RDI: 6% calcium, 26% iron, 37% vit A, 122% vit C, 31% folate.

Grilled Chicken Barley Salad

HANDS-ON TIME		TOTAL TIME		MAKES
10 MINUTES	•	50 MINUTES	•	4 SERVINGS

What you need

2	boneless skinless chicken breasts
⅔ cup	pearl barley
1½ cups	chopped green beans
1 cup	grape tomatoes, halved
¼ cup	minced red onion
2 tbsp	chopped fresh basil

ITALIAN HERB VINAIGRETTE:

¼ cup	extra-virgin olive oil
2 tbsp	wine vinegar
1 tbsp	Dijon mustard
½ tsp	dried Italian herb seasoning
¼ tsp	each salt and pepper

How to make it

ITALIAN HERB VINAIGRETTE: In large bowl, whisk together oil, vinegar, mustard, Italian herb seasoning, salt and pepper. Transfer 2 tbsp to large shallow dish; add chicken, turning to coat. Cover and refrigerate for 10 minutes. *(Make-ahead: Refrigerate for up to 8 hours.)*

Meanwhile, in saucepan of boiling water, cover and cook barley for 15 minutes. Add green beans; cook until beans are tender-crisp and barley is tender, about 5 minutes. Drain; toss with remaining vinaigrette.

Place chicken on greased grill over medium-high heat; close lid and grill, turning once, until no longer pink inside, about 10 minutes. Cut into cubes.

Add chicken to barley mixture. Add tomatoes, red onion and basil; toss to coat.

NUTRITIONAL INFORMATION, PER SERVING: about 340 cal, 19 g pro, 15 g total fat (2 g sat. fat), 33 g carb, 4 g fibre, 39 mg chol, 236 mg sodium. % RDI: 4% calcium, 16% iron, 7% vit A, 13% vit C, 16% folate.

Mediterranean Orzo Salad

HANDS-ON TIME	TOTAL TIME	MAKES
15 MINUTES	20 MINUTES	6 TO 8 SERVINGS

What you need

2 cups	orzo pasta
¼ cup	lemon juice
¼ cup	extra-virgin olive oil
1 tsp	liquid honey
½ tsp	each salt and pepper
pinch	dried oregano
1	sweet red pepper, diced
1 cup	diced cored English cucumber
¾ cup	crumbled feta cheese
⅓ cup	chopped Kalamata olives
⅓ cup	chopped drained oil-packed sun-dried tomatoes
¼ cup	chopped fresh parsley
¼ cup	diced red onion

How to make it

In large pot of boiling lightly salted water, cook orzo according to package directions until al dente. Drain and rinse under cold water; drain well.

In large bowl, whisk together lemon juice, oil, honey, salt, pepper and oregano. Add orzo, red pepper, cucumber, feta cheese, olives, sun-dried tomatoes, parsley and red onion; stir to coat. (*Make-ahead: Cover and refrigerate for up to 24 hours.*)

TIP FROM THE TEST KITCHEN
Stir the finished salad lightly with a fork before serving to loosen the pasta.

NUTRITIONAL INFORMATION, PER EACH OF 8 SERVINGS:
about 286 cal, 8 g pro, 12 g total fat (3 g sat. fat), 37 g carb, 3 g fibre, 13 mg chol, 514 mg sodium, 194 mg potassium. % RDI: 8% calcium, 8% iron, 9% vit A, 63% vit C, 10% folate.

Roasted Pepper and Cheese Tortellini Salad

HANDS-ON TIME	TOTAL TIME	MAKES
15 MINUTES	30 MINUTES	4 SERVINGS

What you need

2	sweet red and/or yellow peppers
1	sweet green pepper
1	pkg (350 g) fresh cheese tortellini
3 tbsp	red wine vinegar
3 tbsp	extra-virgin olive oil
1	clove garlic, minced
½ tsp	dried thyme
½ tsp	Dijon mustard
pinch	each salt and pepper
pinch	hot pepper flakes
¼ cup	pine nuts, toasted (see tip, below)

How to make it

On foil-lined rimmed baking sheet, broil red and green peppers, turning occasionally, until skins are blackened, about 15 minutes. Let cool enough to handle. Peel off blackened skins; core and seed peppers. Cut into ¾-inch (2 cm) pieces.

Meanwhile, in large pot of boiling water, cook tortellini according to package directions; drain. Set aside.

In large bowl, whisk together vinegar, oil, garlic, thyme, mustard, salt, pepper and hot pepper flakes. Stir in peppers, tortellini and pine nuts to coat. *(Make-ahead: Refrigerate in airtight container for up to 2 days.)*

TIP FROM THE TEST KITCHEN
Toast the pine nuts in a small dry skillet over medium-high heat, shaking the pan constantly, until golden, about 3 minutes.

NUTRITIONAL INFORMATION, PER SERVING: about 508 cal, 13 g pro, 22 g total fat (5 g sat. fat), 61 g carb, 5 g fibre, 49 mg chol, 984 mg sodium. % RDI: 10% calcium, 19% iron, 22% vit A, 198% vit C, 8% folate.

Tangy Macaroni Salad

HANDS-ON TIME	•	TOTAL TIME	•	MAKES
15 MINUTES		1½ HOURS		12 SERVINGS

What you need | How to make it

4 cups	elbow macaroni
1 cup	diced celery
¼ cup	chopped drained pimientos

SHALLOT DRESSING:

½ cup	finely chopped shallots or green onions
¼ cup	white wine vinegar
¾ tsp	salt
⅔ cup	mayonnaise
1 tbsp	granulated sugar
2 tsp	Dijon mustard
¼ tsp	pepper

SHALLOT DRESSING: In large bowl, combine shallots, vinegar and salt; let stand for 10 minutes. Stir in mayonnaise, sugar, mustard and pepper.

Meanwhile, in large pot of boiling salted water, cook pasta according to package directions until al dente. Drain and rinse under cold water; drain well.

Add pasta, celery and pimientos to dressing; toss to coat evenly. Cover and refrigerate for 1 hour. (*Make-ahead: Refrigerate for up to 24 hours.*)

NUTRITIONAL INFORMATION, PER SERVING: about 230 cal, 5 g pro, 10 g total fat (2 g sat. fat), 29 g carb, 2 g fibre, 5 mg chol, 325 mg sodium, 90 mg potassium. % RDI: 2% calcium, 11% iron, 3% vit A, 10% vit C, 35% folate.

Mediterranean Fusilli Salad

HANDS-ON TIME	•	TOTAL TIME	•	MAKES
10 MINUTES		20 MINUTES		12 SERVINGS

What you need

4 cups	fusilli pasta
1	zucchini, cubed
1	can (540 mL) romano beans, drained and rinsed
⅔ cup	sliced drained oil-packed sun-dried tomatoes (see tip, below)
¾ cup	thinly sliced fresh basil

CUMIN AND OREGANO DRESSING:

⅔ cup	extra-virgin olive oil
¼ cup	red wine vinegar
1	clove garlic, minced
1 tsp	ground cumin
1 tsp	dried oregano
¼ tsp	each salt and pepper

How to make it

CUMIN AND OREGANO DRESSING: Whisk together oil, vinegar, garlic, cumin, oregano, salt and pepper; set aside.

In large pot of boiling salted water, cook pasta according to package directions until al dente. Drain and rinse under cold water; drain well. Place in large bowl.

Add zucchini, romano beans and sun-dried tomatoes; pour dressing over top. Toss to coat. (*Make-ahead: Cover and refrigerate for up to 24 hours.*)

Just before serving, toss with basil.

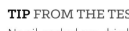

TIP FROM THE TEST KITCHEN
No oil-packed sun-dried tomatoes on hand? No problem. Place dry-packed sun-dried tomatoes in a bowl and pour boiling water over them. Let them stand until they're softened and pliable, about 15 minutes. Drain, slice and add them to recipes as directed. The soaked dried tomatoes will be a little chewier than the jarred ones, but they will be just as sweet.

NUTRITIONAL INFORMATION, PER SERVING: about 263 cal, 6 g pro, 14 g total fat (2 g sat. fat), 30 g carb, 4 g fibre, 0 mg chol, 252 mg sodium. % RDI: 3% calcium, 16% iron, 3% vit A, 15% vit C, 41% folate.

Tuna Pasta Salad

HANDS-ON TIME	•	TOTAL TIME	•	MAKES
20 MINUTES		4½ HOURS		6 TO 8 SERVINGS

What you need

1	large carrot
2	ribs celery
3 cups	medium shell pasta
2	cans (each 170 g) tuna packed in vegetable broth and oil, drained
½ cup	frozen peas, cooked and cooled
½ cup	chopped dill pickles
¼ cup	diced red onion

LEMON DIJON DRESSING:

3 tbsp	lemon juice
3 tbsp	white wine vinegar
1	small clove garlic, minced
1 tsp	Dijon mustard
pinch	each salt and pepper
¼ cup	extra-virgin olive oil

How to make it

Cut carrot in half lengthwise; cut carrot and celery into 4-inch (10 cm) lengths. In large pot of boiling salted water, cook carrot until tender-crisp, about 4 minutes. Using slotted spoon, remove from water; let cool. Add celery to pot; cook for 30 seconds. Using slotted spoon, remove from water; let cool. Thinly slice carrot and celery; set aside.

In same pot of boiling water, cook pasta according to package directions until al dente. Drain and rinse under cold water; drain well. Set aside.

In large bowl, break tuna into chunks; add pasta, carrot, celery, peas, pickles and red onion.

LEMON DIJON DRESSING: Whisk together lemon juice, vinegar, garlic, mustard, salt and pepper; slowly whisk in oil until emulsified. Add to pasta mixture; toss to coat. Cover and refrigerate for 4 hours. (*Make-ahead: Refrigerate for up to 2 days.*)

TIP FROM THE TEST KITCHEN
Onions can be potent, especially when they're added raw to salads. To make them milder, soak slices or pieces in cold water for 30 minutes. Drain well and add to the salad as directed.

NUTRITIONAL INFORMATION, PER EACH OF 8 SERVINGS: about 234 cal, 13 g pro, 8 g total fat (1 g sat. fat), 27 g carb, 2 g fibre, 15 mg chol, 358 mg sodium. % RDI: 2% calcium, 12% iron, 21% vit A, 8% vit C, 33% folate.

Salmon Pasta Salad

HANDS-ON TIME	TOTAL TIME	MAKES
10 MINUTES	20 MINUTES	4 SERVINGS

What you need

4 cups	small shell pasta
1 cup	frozen peas
1	can (213 g) sockeye salmon, drained
½ cup	low-fat plain yogurt
⅓ cup	finely diced red onion
¼ cup	light mayonnaise
6	radishes, thinly sliced
2 tbsp	chopped fresh dill
½ tsp	each salt and pepper
½ tsp	hot pepper sauce
12	leaves romaine lettuce

How to make it

In large saucepan of boiling salted water, cook pasta according to package directions until al dente, adding peas during last 1 minute of cooking. Drain and rinse under cold water; drain well, shaking to remove excess water from insides of shells.

Meanwhile, flake salmon with fork, mashing in any bones; remove skin, if desired. Set aside.

In large bowl, stir together yogurt, red onion, mayonnaise, radishes, dill, salt, pepper and hot pepper sauce.

Tear 4 of the lettuce leaves into bite-size pieces; add to dressing along with pasta mixture and salmon. Toss to combine.

Line 4 plates with remaining lettuce leaves; spoon salad onto lettuce.

NUTRITIONAL INFORMATION, PER SERVING: about 484 cal, 24 g pro, 10 g total fat (2 g sat. fat), 74 g carb, 6 g fibre, 26 mg chol, 985 mg sodium. % RDI: 18% calcium, 24% iron, 13% vit A, 25% vit C, 87% folate.

Grilled Vegetable and Israeli Couscous Salad

HANDS-ON TIME	•	TOTAL TIME	•	MAKES
30 MINUTES		1½ HOURS		12 SERVINGS

What you need

2 cups	Israeli couscous (see tip, below)
1	eggplant
1¼ tsp	salt
2	zucchini
1	small red onion
2	cloves garlic
½ cup	extra-virgin olive oil
¼ cup	sherry vinegar
¼ tsp	granulated sugar
¼ tsp	pepper
3	portobello mushrooms, stemmed and gills removed (see tip, page 10)
⅓ cup	chopped fresh parsley

How to make it

In saucepan of boiling salted water, cook couscous according to package directions. Drain and rinse under cold water; drain well. Transfer to large bowl.

Meanwhile, slice eggplant; in colander, toss eggplant with ¼ tsp of the salt. Let drain for 10 minutes. Pat dry with paper towel.

Meanwhile, slice zucchini lengthwise. Slice red onion crosswise into ½-inch (1 cm) thick rounds.

Finely chop garlic. Add a pinch of the remaining salt; using flat side of chef's knife, rub into paste. Stir together garlic paste, oil, vinegar, sugar, pepper and remaining salt. Lightly brush some over eggplant, zucchini, red onion and mushrooms.

Place vegetables on greased grill over medium heat; close lid and grill, turning often, until tender, 7 to 10 minutes. Cut into 1-inch (2.5 cm) pieces; add to couscous.

Add remaining oil mixture and parsley to couscous mixture; toss to coat. Let stand for 1 hour. *(Make-ahead: Refrigerate for up to 24 hours.)*

TIP FROM THE TEST KITCHEN

If you don't have any Israeli couscous, substitute orzo, ditalini, acini di pepe or small shell pasta.

NUTRITIONAL INFORMATION, PER SERVING: about 212 cal, 5 g pro, 10 g total fat (1 g sat. fat), 27 g carb, 3 g fibre, 0 mg chol, 226 mg sodium, 346 mg potassium. % RDI: 2% calcium, 6% iron, 5% vit A, 8% vit C, 15% folate.

Thai Beef Noodle Salad

HANDS-ON TIME	•	TOTAL TIME	•	MAKES
20 MINUTES		4¾ HOURS		4 TO 6 SERVINGS

What you need

1	piece (8 inches/20 cm long) English cucumber
1	large carrot
175 g	rice stick noodles (about ⅓ inch/8 mm) wide
quarter	red onion, thinly sliced
3 tbsp	each chopped fresh cilantro and mint
3 tbsp	Thai or other basil leaves
¼ cup	chopped unsalted peanuts

MARINATED STEAK:

2 tbsp	grated fresh ginger
2 tbsp	soy sauce
2	cloves garlic, minced
1 tbsp	granulated sugar
1 tbsp	each sesame oil and vegetable oil
1	beef flank marinating steak (about 450 g)

DRESSING:

½ cup	hot water
¼ cup	granulated sugar
2 tbsp	lime juice
2 tbsp	fish sauce
2	Thai bird's-eye peppers or serrano chilies, seeded and thinly sliced

How to make it

MARINATED STEAK: In glass baking dish, combine ginger, soy sauce, garlic, sugar, sesame oil and vegetable oil; add steak, turning to coat. Cover and refrigerate for 4 hours, turning occasionally. *(Make-ahead: Refrigerate for up to 12 hours.)*

DRESSING: In jar with tight-fitting lid, shake hot water with sugar until dissolved. Add lime juice, fish sauce and Thai peppers; shake to combine. *(Make-ahead: Refrigerate for up to 5 days.)*

Using vegetable peeler, slice cucumber lengthwise into thin strips, slicing around and discarding centre seeds; set aside. Slice carrot lengthwise into thin strips; set aside.

In large pot of boiling salted water, cook rice noodles according to package directions. Drain and rinse under cold water; drain well. In large bowl, toss noodles with dressing; set aside.

Discarding marinade, place steak on greased grill over medium-high heat; close lid and grill, turning once, until medium-rare, about 8 minutes. Transfer to cutting board and tent with foil; let stand for 5 minutes before thinly slicing across the grain.

Add cucumber, carrot, red onion, cilantro, mint and basil to noodle mixture; toss to coat. Divide among bowls or plates; top with steak. Sprinkle with peanuts.

NUTRITIONAL INFORMATION, PER EACH OF 6 SERVINGS:
about 363 cal, 21 g pro, 13 g total fat (3 g sat. fat), 41 g carb, 3 g fibre, 31 mg chol, 873 mg sodium. % RDI: 4% calcium, 15% iron, 26% vit A, 20% vit C, 14% folate.

Japanese Noodle Salad

HANDS-ON TIME	•	TOTAL TIME	•	MAKES
15 MINUTES		30 MINUTES		4 SERVINGS

What you need

1	pkg (340 g) chuka soba noodles or ramen noodles
2	eggs
1	green onion (dark green part only)
1 tsp	vegetable oil
1 cup	shredded romaine lettuce
half	English cucumber, julienned
2	plum tomatoes, quartered
1 tbsp	toasted sesame seeds

SESAME SHIITAKE DRESSING:

1	pkg (7 g) dried shiitake mushrooms
1 cup	boiling water
3 tbsp	unseasoned rice vinegar
2 tbsp	soy sauce
4 tsp	granulated sugar
1 tsp	sesame oil

How to make it

SESAME SHIITAKE DRESSING: In glass measure, soak mushrooms in boiling water until softened, about 10 minutes. Reserving liquid, remove mushrooms and pat dry; thinly slice. Strain liquid into small bowl; add vinegar, soy sauce, sugar and sesame oil. Set aside.

Meanwhile, cook noodles according to package directions. Drain and rinse under cold water; drain well. Pat dry.

In small bowl, beat eggs with 1 tsp water; stir in green onion. In nonstick skillet, heat oil over medium-low heat; pour in egg mixture and cook, without stirring, to make thin omelette. Transfer to cutting board; thinly slice.

Divide noodles among 4 plates. Surround with piles of lettuce, cucumber, tomatoes, eggs and mushrooms. Sprinkle with sesame seeds. Serve each plate with small dish of dressing to pour over top.

TIP FROM THE TEST KITCHEN

If you like ginger, garnish this salad with red beni shoga, a pungent shredded pickled ginger that's dyed bright red. If you can't find it in an Asian grocery store, try pink or natural sushi ginger instead.

NUTRITIONAL INFORMATION, PER SERVING: about 399 cal, 20 g pro, 6 g total fat (1 g sat. fat), 73 g carb, 5 g fibre, 93 mg chol, 949 mg sodium. % RDI: 4% calcium, 18% iron, 7% vit A, 10% vit C, 25% folate.

Korean Cold Somen Noodle Salad

HANDS-ON TIME	•	TOTAL TIME	•	MAKES
20 MINUTES		45 MINUTES		4 TO 6 SERVINGS

What you need

275 g	somen noodles
half	English cucumber, halved lengthwise, cored and sliced
125 g	deli sliced ham (optional), julienned
1½ cups	sliced cored Asian pear
1 cup	kimchi, chopped
½ cup	finely chopped green onion
¼ cup	kimchi juice (see tip, below)
4 cups	shredded frisée or red leaf lettuce
1	sheet roasted nori, cut in strips

PICKLED DAIKON:

½ cup	thinly sliced peeled daikon
1 tbsp	unseasoned rice vinegar
½ tsp	granulated sugar

SAUCE:

3 tbsp	Korean hot pepper paste (gochujang)
3 tbsp	unseasoned rice vinegar
2 tbsp	toasted sesame seeds
2 tbsp	sesame oil
4 tsp	granulated sugar
1 tbsp	sodium-reduced soy sauce

How to make it

PICKLED DAIKON: Combine daikon, vinegar and sugar; refrigerate for 15 minutes.

SAUCE: Meanwhile, stir together hot pepper paste, vinegar, sesame seeds, sesame oil, sugar and soy sauce; set aside.

Meanwhile, in large pot of boiling water, cook noodles according to package directions. Drain and rinse under cold running water until no longer starchy. Drain well; shake to remove excess water. Set aside to dry for 10 minutes.

In bowl, combine noodles, cucumber, ham (if using), pear, kimchi, green onion and kimchi juice; add half of the sauce and toss to combine.

Add frisée, tossing gently; sprinkle with nori. Divide among bowls; top with pickled daikon. Serve remaining sauce on the side.

TIP FROM THE TEST KITCHEN
To make kimchi juice, gently squeeze the kimchi and top it up with some of the brine from the jar if necessary

NUTRITIONAL INFORMATION, PER EACH OF 6 SERVINGS:
about 257 cal, 6 g pro, 7 g total fat (1 g sat. fat), 43 g carb, 6 g fibre, 0 mg chol, 908 mg sodium, 269 mg potassium. % RDI: 4% calcium, 12% iron, 22% vit A, 23% vit C, 30% folate.

Rice Vermicelli Salad With Vietnamese Pork Chops

HANDS-ON TIME	TOTAL TIME	MAKES
20 MINUTES	50 MINUTES	4 SERVINGS

What you need

125 g	rice stick vermicelli
2 cups	shredded leaf lettuce
½ cup	finely grated carrot
¼ cup	each shredded fresh mint and cilantro
¼ cup	chopped roasted peanuts (optional)

VIETNAMESE PORK CHOPS:

½ cup	finely chopped shallots or onion
3 tbsp	packed brown sugar
2 tbsp	each lime juice and fish sauce
1 tbsp	vegetable oil
½ tsp	pepper
4	boneless pork loin centre chops, trimmed

DRESSING:

3 tbsp	lime juice
1 tbsp	granulated sugar
1 tbsp	boiling water
1 tbsp	fish sauce
1	clove garlic, minced
½ tsp	minced hot pepper

How to make it

VIETNAMESE PORK CHOPS: In bowl, whisk together shallots, brown sugar, lime juice, fish sauce, oil and pepper; add pork, turning to coat. Cover and marinate for 15 minutes. Pour marinade into small saucepan; set aside.

Place pork on greased grill over medium-high heat; close lid and grill, turning once, until juices run clear when pork is pierced and just a hint of pink remains inside, about 10 minutes. Transfer to plate; tent with foil. Let stand for 5 minutes before thinly slicing.

DRESSING: Meanwhile, stir together lime juice, sugar, boiling water, fish sauce, garlic and hot pepper. Set aside.

In large bowl, soak rice vermicelli according to package directions. Drain and rinse under cold water; drain well, squeezing out excess water. Return rice vermicelli to bowl; add dressing, lettuce, carrot, mint and cilantro. Toss to coat.

Meanwhile, bring reserved marinade to boil over high heat; reduce heat and simmer until syrupy, 4 to 5 minutes.

Arrange salad on 4 plates; top with pork. Sprinkle with peanuts (if using); serve with sauce.

NUTRITIONAL INFORMATION, PER SERVING: about 346 cal, 24 g pro, 6 g total fat (1 g sat. fat), 47 g carb, 3 g fibre, 45 mg chol, 812 mg sodium, 540 mg potassium. % RDI: 5% calcium, 15% iron, 42% vit A, 17% vit C, 18% folate.

Coleslaw With
Cider Vinaigrette
page 121

Smashed Potato Salad
opposite

Smashed Potato Salad

HANDS-ON TIME	TOTAL TIME	MAKES
35 MINUTES	2 HOURS	8 SERVINGS

What you need

4	large white potatoes (about 750 g), peeled
3	hard-cooked eggs (see tip, page 19), chopped
half	Vidalia or other sweet onion, finely chopped
2	ribs celery, diced
½ cup	diced gherkin pickles (see tip, below)
½ cup	mayonnaise
2 tbsp	Dijon mustard
1 tbsp	cider vinegar
¾ tsp	salt
½ tsp	pepper
¼ tsp	sweet paprika

How to make it

In large pot of boiling salted water, cook potatoes until fork-tender, about 15 minutes. Drain and coarsely chop; place in large bowl.

Add eggs, onion, celery and pickles to potatoes, breaking up slightly with potato masher.

Whisk together mayonnaise, mustard, vinegar, salt, pepper and paprika. Add to potato mixture; mix well. Cover and refrigerate until chilled, about 1 hour. *(Make-ahead: Refrigerate for up to 24 hours.)*

TIP FROM THE TEST KITCHEN

Sweet or sour gherkin pickles work equally well in this salad. Choose according to the level of tanginess you prefer.

NUTRITIONAL INFORMATION, PER SERVING: about 208 cal, 4 g pro, 13 g total fat (2 g sat. fat), 20 g carb, 2 g fibre, 75 mg chol, 634 mg sodium, 315 mg potassium. % RDI: 3% calcium, 6% iron, 5% vit A, 12% vit C, 11% folate.

Warm Potato Salad With Chorizo

HANDS-ON TIME
15 MINUTES

TOTAL TIME
40 MINUTES

MAKES
4 SERVINGS

What you need

900 g	yellow-fleshed potatoes, scrubbed
3	eggs
2 tbsp	olive oil
1	dry-cured chorizo sausage (see tip, below), sliced
1	onion, diced
¾ cup	vegetable broth
¼ cup	white wine vinegar
½ cup	chopped green onions
2 tbsp	grainy mustard
¼ tsp	each salt and pepper

How to make it

In large pot of boiling salted water, cook potatoes until fork-tender, 20 to 25 minutes. Drain; let cool enough to handle. Cut into thick slices; transfer to large bowl.

Meanwhile, in separate saucepan, arrange eggs in single layer; pour in enough cold water to cover by 1 inch (2.5 cm). Bring to boil. Remove from heat; cover and let stand for 12 minutes. Drain and chill under cold water. Drain, peel off shells and thinly slice; add to potatoes.

Meanwhile, in large skillet, heat oil over medium heat; cook chorizo, stirring often, until browned, 3 to 4 minutes. Using slotted spoon, add to potato mixture.

Add onion to pan; cook, stirring occasionally, until golden, 6 to 8 minutes. Add broth and vinegar; bring to boil. Pour over potato mixture. Add green onions, mustard, salt and pepper; toss gently to coat.

TIP FROM THE TEST KITCHEN

There are two types of chorizo. Dry-cured doesn't have to be cooked before eating (although browning the slices makes them crispy). Fresh chorizo contains raw meat, is milder than dry-cured chorizo and must be cooked before eating. The two types aren't interchangeable in recipes.

NUTRITIONAL INFORMATION, PER SERVING: about 376 cal, 13 g pro, 17 g total fat (4 g sat. fat), 43 g carb, 4 g fibre, 176 mg chol, 1,076 mg sodium, 917 mg potassium. % RDI: 6% calcium, 20% iron, 8% vit A, 42% vit C, 21% folate.

Fully Loaded Potato Salad

HANDS-ON TIME	•	TOTAL TIME	•	MAKES
45 MINUTES		1½ HOURS		6 TO 8 SERVINGS

What you need

1.5 kg	white potatoes (about 7), scrubbed
1 cup	light sour cream
¾ cup	light mayonnaise
½ tsp	each salt and pepper
¾ cup	crumbled blue cheese
4	slices thick-cut bacon
3 tbsp	chopped fresh chives (see tip, below)

How to make it

In large pot of boiling salted water, cook potatoes until tender, about 25 minutes. Drain and let cool slightly; peel. Refrigerate until completely cool; cut into chunks.

In large bowl, stir together sour cream, mayonnaise, salt and pepper. Add potatoes; toss to coat. Add blue cheese; gently toss to combine. (*Make-ahead: Cover and refrigerate for up to 24 hours.*)

Meanwhile, in large skillet, cook bacon over medium heat, turning once, until crisp, about 8 minutes. Drain on paper towel–lined plate; let cool slightly. Chop.

To serve, sprinkle bacon and chives over salad.

TIP FROM THE TEST KITCHEN
Substitute very thinly sliced green onions for the chives if you like a more assertive onion flavour.

NUTRITIONAL INFORMATION, PER EACH OF 8 SERVINGS:
about 305 cal, 9 g pro, 14 g total fat (5 g sat. fat), 36 g carb, 2 g fibre, 26 mg chol, 951 mg sodium, 718 mg potassium. % RDI: 12% calcium, 5% iron, 5% vit A, 33% vit C, 10% folate.

Potato Persillade Salad

HANDS-ON TIME	TOTAL TIME	MAKES
10 MINUTES	35 MINUTES	8 SERVINGS

What you need

1.35 kg	potatoes, peeled
4	green onions, thinly sliced

PERSILLADE SAUCE:

1 cup	loosely packed fresh parsley leaves
⅓ cup	extra-virgin olive oil
1	clove garlic, minced
2 tbsp	lemon juice
½ tsp	each salt and pepper

How to make it

PERSILLADE SAUCE: In food processor, chop together parsley, oil, garlic, lemon juice, salt and pepper until almost smooth. Set aside.

In large pot of boiling salted water, cook potatoes until tender, 20 to 25 minutes. Drain; let cool slightly. Cut potatoes into chunks.

In bowl, toss potatoes with green onions. Pour sauce over top; toss to coat.

TIP FROM THE TEST KITCHEN

Persillade is a savoury parsley-based sauce that's delicious on more than just these potatoes. Combine it with fresh bread crumbs to make a crispy herbed topping for roasted meats; simply spread the mixture over a rack of lamb or a pork roast before sliding it into the oven. Persillade also makes a tasty sauce for fish.

NUTRITIONAL INFORMATION, PER SERVING: about 203 cal, 3 g pro, 9 g total fat (1 g sat. fat), 29 g carb, 2 g fibre, 0 mg chol, 478 mg sodium. % RDI: 3% calcium, 8% iron, 7% vit A, 38% vit C, 13% folate.

Rainbow Slaw

HANDS-ON TIME	•	TOTAL TIME	•	MAKES
15 MINUTES		2¼ HOURS		8 SERVINGS

What you need

1	red-skinned apple (such as Spartan or Empire) or Granny Smith apple
1½ tsp	lemon juice
2 cups	shredded green cabbage
2 cups	shredded red cabbage
½ cup	sliced celery
¼ cup	chopped toasted walnuts (see tip, below)
¼ cup	light sour cream
4 tsp	cider vinegar
¼ tsp	pepper
dash	hot pepper sauce
pinch	each salt and celery salt
⅓ cup	crumbled blue cheese

How to make it

Halve and core apple; julienne. In large bowl, toss apple with lemon juice. Add green and red cabbage, celery and walnuts.

Whisk together sour cream, vinegar, pepper, hot pepper sauce, salt and celery salt; pour over cabbage mixture. Toss to combine. Refrigerate for 2 hours. *(Make-ahead: Cover and refrigerate for up to 24 hours.)*

Just before serving, sprinkle salad with blue cheese.

TIP FROM THE TEST KITCHEN

To toast the walnuts, spread them on a rimmed baking sheet and toast in a 350°F (180°C) oven until they're light golden, 6 to 8 minutes. Let them cool before adding them to the salad.

NUTRITIONAL INFORMATION, PER SERVING: about 73 cal, 3 g pro, 5 g total fat (2 g sat. fat), 7 g carb, 1 g fibre, 5 mg chol, 96 mg sodium. % RDI: 6% calcium, 3% iron, 2% vit A, 28% vit C, 9% folate.

Kohlrabi and Rutabaga Slaw

HANDS-ON TIME	•	TOTAL TIME	•	MAKES
15 MINUTES		15 MINUTES		4 TO 6 SERVINGS

What you need

¼ cup	light mayonnaise
¼ cup	Balkan-style plain yogurt
1 tbsp	lemon juice
2 tsp	Dijon mustard
¼ tsp	each salt and pepper
2 cups	julienned peeled trimmed kohlrabi
2 cups	julienned peeled rutabaga
¼ cup	chopped fresh parsley

How to make it

In large bowl, whisk together mayonnaise, yogurt, lemon juice, mustard, salt and pepper.

Add kohlrabi, rutabaga and parsley; toss to coat. *(Make-ahead: Refrigerate in airtight container for up to 3 days. Toss before serving.)*

NUTRITIONAL INFORMATION, PER EACH OF 6 SERVINGS:
about 70 cal, 2 g pro, 4 g total fat (1 g sat. fat), 8 g carb, 3 g fibre, 5 mg chol, 208 mg sodium, 325 mg potassium. % RDI: 5% calcium, 4% iron, 3% vit A, 63% vit C, 9% folate.

Coleslaw
With Cider Vinaigrette

HANDS-ON TIME	TOTAL TIME	MAKES
15 MINUTES	2¼ HOURS	10 TO 12 SERVINGS

What you need

10 cups	shredded green cabbage
1½ cups	thinly sliced radishes
half	Vidalia or other sweet onion, thinly sliced
2 tbsp	chopped fresh parsley

CIDER VINAIGRETTE:

¼ cup	cider vinegar
1 tbsp	lemon juice
2 tsp	granulated sugar
½ tsp	salt
¼ tsp	pepper
⅓ cup	extra-virgin olive oil

How to make it

CIDER VINAIGRETTE: In large bowl, whisk together vinegar, lemon juice, sugar, salt and pepper until sugar is dissolved, about 1 minute. Whisk in oil until blended.

Add cabbage, radishes, onion and parsley; toss to coat. Cover and refrigerate for 2 hours. (*Make-ahead: Refrigerate for up to 24 hours.*)

VARIATION

Tropical Coleslaw
Substitute lime juice for the vinegar in the vinaigrette, and fresh cilantro for the parsley in the vegetable mixture. Add 1 cup diced peeled cored pineapple and 1 mango, peeled, pitted and diced.

TIP FROM THE TEST KITCHEN
This is a salad that actually gets better the longer it stands. For maximum deliciousness, make it a day before you plan to serve it.

NUTRITIONAL INFORMATION, PER EACH OF 12 SERVINGS:
about 78 cal, 1 g pro, 6 g total fat (1 g sat. fat), 6 g carb, 1 g fibre, 0 mg chol, 114 mg sodium, 204 mg potassium. % RDI: 3% calcium, 4% iron, 2% vit A, 38% vit C, 15% folate.

Macadamia Nut Slaw

HANDS-ON TIME	•	TOTAL TIME	•	MAKES
15 MINUTES		15 MINUTES		8 SERVINGS

What you need

quarter	head each napa cabbage and red cabbage
2	small carrots
2	green onions
1	Asian or Bosc pear, peeled, halved and cored
half	sweet red pepper
½ cup	chopped macadamia nuts
3 tbsp	chopped fresh mint

CHILI GINGER DRESSING:

¼ cup	vegetable oil
¼ cup	unseasoned rice vinegar
4 tsp	lime juice
2 tsp	finely grated fresh ginger
½ tsp	sweet Asian chili sauce
¼ tsp	salt

How to make it

CHILI GINGER DRESSING: Whisk together oil, vinegar, lime juice, ginger, chili sauce and salt; set aside.

Thinly slice napa and red cabbages; place in large bowl. Julienne carrots, green onions, pear and red pepper; add to bowl. Pour dressing over top; toss to coat. *(Make-ahead: Cover and refrigerate for up to 6 hours.)*

Just before serving, sprinkle with macadamia nuts and mint.

TIP FROM THE TEST KITCHEN
If you don't have any sweet Asian chili sauce, use ½ tsp hot pepper sauce mixed with ¼ tsp granulated sugar.

NUTRITIONAL INFORMATION, PER SERVING: about 156 cal, 2 g pro, 14 g total fat (2 g sat. fat), 10 g carb, 3 g fibre, 0 mg chol, 93 mg sodium. % RDI: 5% calcium, 6% iron, 23% vit A, 70% vit C, 19% folate.

Heirloom Carrot Salad

HANDS-ON TIME	TOTAL TIME	MAKES
15 MINUTES	15 MINUTES	4 SERVINGS

What you need

450 g	multicoloured heirloom carrots (about 3)
12	sprigs fresh cilantro
¼ cup	toasted unsalted pepitas (see tip, below)
¼ cup	crumbled feta cheese

ORANGE CUMIN VINAIGRETTE:

¼ tsp	cumin seeds, crushed
2 tbsp	orange juice
1 tbsp	vegetable oil
1 tbsp	lemon juice
½ tsp	ground coriander
½ tsp	liquid honey
pinch	each salt and pepper

How to make it

Using mandoline or vegetable peeler, slice carrots lengthwise into paper-thin strips. Place carrots and cilantro in bowl of ice water; let stand for 3 minutes. Drain and pat dry.

ORANGE CUMIN VINAIGRETTE: Meanwhile, in small dry skillet over medium-high heat, toast cumin seeds until darkened and just beginning to pop, about 30 seconds. Transfer to large bowl. Whisk in orange juice, oil, lemon juice, coriander, honey, salt and pepper.

Add carrots, cilantro and pepitas to vinaigrette; toss to coat. Sprinkle with feta cheese.

TIP FROM THE TEST KITCHEN
Pepitas are hulled green pumpkin seeds and are the richest natural source of magnesium. They are available raw, roasted, unsalted and salted. Look for them in supermarkets, bulk and natural foods stores, and Latin American markets.

NUTRITIONAL INFORMATION, PER SERVING: about 185 cal, 7 g pro, 12 g total fat (3 g sat. fat), 15 g carb, 5 g fibre, 9 mg chol, 190 mg sodium, 542 mg potassium. % RDI: 9% calcium, 20% iron, 196% vit A, 22% vit C, 19% folate.

Fiddlehead, Pea and Asparagus Salad With Mint Vinaigrette

HANDS-ON TIME	TOTAL TIME	MAKES
25 MINUTES	25 MINUTES	4 SERVINGS

What you need

1 cup	fresh or frozen peas
12	spears asparagus, trimmed (see tip, page 16) and cut in 5-inch (12 cm) lengths
3 cups	fiddleheads (about 280 g), cleaned (see tip, below)
¼ cup	crumbled soft goat cheese

MINT VINAIGRETTE:

3 tbsp	extra-virgin olive oil
2 tbsp	lemon juice
¼ tsp	granulated sugar
pinch	each salt and pepper
¼ cup	packed fresh mint leaves, chopped

How to make it

In large pot of boiling salted water, blanch peas until tender, 1 to 4 minutes. Using slotted spoon, transfer to bowl of ice water; set aside.

In same pot, blanch asparagus until tender-crisp, about 3 minutes. Using slotted spoon, add to peas. In same pot, blanch fiddleheads for 5 minutes. Drain; add to peas. Let cool.

Drain fiddlehead mixture and pat dry. Halve asparagus pieces crosswise.

MINT VINAIGRETTE: In large bowl, whisk together oil, lemon juice, sugar, salt and pepper; stir in mint.

Add fiddlehead mixture to vinaigrette; toss to coat. Sprinkle with goat cheese.

TIP FROM THE TEST KITCHEN

To clean fiddleheads, snap off the bright green tops, leaving 2 inches (5 cm) of the stems attached. Discard remaining stems. Rub off the dry brown casings. Soak fiddleheads in a sink half-full of cold water, changing the water several times to remove any grit or casing particles. Drain well.

NUTRITIONAL INFORMATION, PER SERVING: about 188 cal, 9 g pro, 13 g total fat (3 g sat. fat), 13 g carb, 4 g fibre, 4 mg chol, 437 mg sodium. % RDI: 7% calcium, 21% iron, 42% vit A, 45% vit C, 44% folate.

Three-Pea Salad

HANDS-ON TIME
15 MINUTES
•
TOTAL TIME
15 MINUTES
•
MAKES
6 SERVINGS

What you need

1 cup	shelled fresh peas
450 g	sugar snap peas, trimmed
2 tbsp	white balsamic vinegar or wine vinegar
2 tsp	liquid honey
pinch	each salt and pepper
¼ cup	extra-virgin olive oil
6	radishes, thinly sliced
3	green onions, thinly sliced
4 cups	trimmed fresh pea tendrils (see tip, below) or watercress
¾ cup	crumbled feta cheese

How to make it

In saucepan of boiling salted water, cook shelled peas for 1½ minutes. Add sugar snap peas; cook just until tender, about 1 minute. Drain and transfer to bowl of ice water; let cool. Drain well; set aside.

In small bowl, whisk together vinegar, honey, salt and pepper; whisk in oil. *(Make-ahead: Refrigerate peas and dressing in separate airtight containers for up to 24 hours. Bring to room temperature.)*

In large bowl, combine shelled peas, snap peas, radishes, green onions and pea tendrils; toss with dressing to coat. Add feta cheese; toss to coat.

TIP FROM THE TEST KITCHEN

In the cool early spring, leafy young tendrils (also called pea shoots) appear on sugar snap pea, snow pea and shelling pea plants. They taste great in salads and make pretty garnishes. You'll often find pea tendrils in Chinese grocery stores in late winter, spring and fall.

NUTRITIONAL INFORMATION, PER SERVING: about 196 cal, 7 g pro, 13 g total fat (4 g sat. fat), 13 g carb, 4 g fibre, 7 mg chol, 444 mg sodium, 365 mg potassium. % RDI: 15% calcium, 15% iron, 23% vit A, 82% vit C, 23% folate.

Carrot and Peanut Salad

HANDS-ON TIME		TOTAL TIME		MAKES
15 MINUTES	•	25 MINUTES	•	8 TO 10 SERVINGS

What you need

¼ cup	peanut oil or vegetable oil
3 tbsp	lime juice
2 tbsp	fish sauce
1 tbsp	granulated sugar
1 tbsp	unseasoned rice vinegar
1 to 3	Thai bird's-eye peppers (or 1 jalapeño pepper), seeded and minced
1	clove garlic, minced
½ tsp	salt
6 cups	shredded carrots
1¼ cups	thinly sliced radishes
¾ cup	unsalted roasted peanuts, coarsely chopped
⅓ cup	chopped fresh cilantro

How to make it

In large bowl, whisk together oil, lime juice, fish sauce, sugar, vinegar, Thai pepper(s), garlic and salt.

Add carrots, radishes, peanuts and cilantro; toss to coat. Let stand for 10 minutes; wearing rubber gloves, tilt bowl and gently press salad to squeeze out excess liquid. Serve immediately or cover and refrigerate for up to 2 hours.

TIP FROM THE TEST KITCHEN
For a more colourful salad, use a mix of heirloom carrots. They come in red, orange, yellow and purple.

NUTRITIONAL INFORMATION, PER EACH OF 10 SERVINGS:
about 144 cal, 4 g pro, 11 g total fat (2 g sat. fat), 11 g carb, 3 g fibre, 0 mg chol, 440 mg sodium, 333 mg potassium. % RDI: 3% calcium, 3% iron, 80% vit A, 14% vit C, 14% folate.

Orange and Beet Salad With Parmesan Curls

HANDS-ON TIME
20 MINUTES

TOTAL TIME
55 MINUTES

MAKES
4 SERVINGS

What you need

4	beets (about 450 g)
3	navel oranges
⅓ cup	walnut pieces
1	piece (60 g) Parmigiano-Reggiano cheese (see tip, below)
2 cups	arugula or watercress, trimmed

WALNUT SHALLOT VINAIGRETTE:

¼ cup	walnut or extra-virgin olive oil
2 tbsp	minced shallot or onion
2 tbsp	wine vinegar
1 tsp	liquid honey
pinch	each salt and pepper

How to make it

WALNUT SHALLOT VINAIGRETTE: Whisk together oil, shallot, vinegar, honey, salt and pepper; set aside. *(Make-ahead: Cover and refrigerate for up to 2 days.)*

Trim off beet tops, leaving 1 inch (2.5 cm) of stems attached; leave roots attached. In saucepan of boiling salted water, cover and cook beets until fork-tender, 25 to 30 minutes. Drain; let cool. Peel beets; cut crosswise into ¼-inch (5 mm) thick slices.

Cut off rind and outer membrane of oranges. Cut oranges crosswise into ¼-inch (5 mm) thick slices. *(Make-ahead: Place beets and oranges in separate bowls; cover and refrigerate for up to 24 hours.)*

In small dry skillet, toast walnuts over medium-low heat, stirring often, until lightly browned, about 3 minutes. Let cool.

Using vegetable peeler, shave Parmigiano-Reggiano cheese into thin curls.

Mound arugula on platter or individual plates. Overlap beets and oranges in centre. Sprinkle with walnuts; drizzle with vinaigrette. Scatter cheese over top.

TIP FROM THE TEST KITCHEN
If real Parmigiano-Reggiano is too pricey, try this salad with more affordable Parmesan or grana Padano cheese.

NUTRITIONAL INFORMATION, PER SERVING: about 348 cal, 10 g pro, 24 g total fat (4 g sat. fat), 27 g carb, 6 g fibre, 12 mg chol, 494 mg sodium. % RDI: 24% calcium, 12% iron, 11% vit A, 113% vit C, 65% folate.

Chayote Salad

HANDS-ON TIME	•	TOTAL TIME	•	MAKES
5 MINUTES		12 MINUTES		6 SERVINGS

What you need

3	small chayotes
3 tbsp	extra-virgin olive oil
2 tbsp	lime juice
half	small clove garlic, finely grated
¼ tsp	each salt and pepper
2 tbsp	chopped fresh cilantro

How to make it

In saucepan of boiling salted water, boil chayotes until tender-crisp, about 5 minutes. Using tongs, transfer to bowl of ice water; let cool. Drain well. Slice thinly; pat dry with paper towels.

In large bowl, whisk together oil, lime juice, garlic, salt and pepper. Add chayote and cilantro; toss to coat.

VARIATION
Zucchini Salad
Substitute 3 small zucchini (450 g) for chayotes; simmer, whole, until tender-crisp, about 7 minutes. Trim off ends; continue with recipe.

TIP FROM THE TEST KITCHEN
You can prepare the chayotes and the dressing ahead and refrigerate them separately for a few hours. Toss them together right before serving to keep the salad from getting watery.

NUTRITIONAL INFORMATION, PER SERVING: about 80 cal, 1 g pro, 7 g total fat (1 g sat. fat), 4 g carb, 2 g fibre, 0 mg chol, 276 mg sodium, 139 mg potassium. % RDI: 1% calcium, 2% iron, 1% vit A, 12% vit C, 6% folate.

Caprese Salad

HANDS-ON TIME	TOTAL TIME	MAKES
15 MINUTES	15 MINUTES	8 SERVINGS

What you need

1⅓ cups	lightly packed fresh basil leaves
¼ cup	extra-virgin olive oil
4 tsp	balsamic vinegar
pinch	each salt and pepper
1	ball (250 g) fresh mozzarella cheese (see tip, below)
4	tomatoes, preferably plum
¼ cup	thinly sliced red onion

How to make it

In food processor or blender, purée ⅓ cup of the basil, oil, vinegar, salt and pepper until smooth. *(Make-ahead: Refrigerate in airtight container for up to 4 hours; shake before using.)*

Cut mozzarella cheese into ¼-inch (5 mm) thick slices. Cut tomatoes into ½-inch (1 cm) thick slices.

On serving platter, alternately layer cheese, tomatoes and remaining basil in concentric circles. Sprinkle with red onion. *(Make-ahead: Cover and refrigerate for up to 4 hours.)*

Just before serving, drizzle dressing over salad.

TIP FROM THE TEST KITCHEN
Fresh mozzarella cheese is moist, snowy white and very soft. Low-moisture mozzarella is drier and yellower; it's a good choice for pizza but not this salad.

NUTRITIONAL INFORMATION, PER SERVING: about 144 cal, 6 g pro, 13 g total fat (5 g sat. fat), 2 g carb, 1 g fibre, 16 mg chol, 39 mg sodium, 113 mg potassium. % RDI: 10% calcium, 3% iron, 13% vit A, 8% vit C, 5% folate.

Heirloom Tomatoes With Basil

HANDS-ON TIME	•	TOTAL TIME	•	MAKES
5 MINUTES		5 MINUTES		6 TO 8 SERVINGS

What you need

900 g	mixed heirloom tomatoes
pinch	each salt and pepper
1 tbsp	extra-virgin olive oil
1 tbsp	wine vinegar
4	leaves fresh basil, shredded

How to make it

Cut tomatoes into ½-inch (1 cm) thick slices; arrange in centre of serving platter.

Sprinkle with salt and pepper; drizzle with oil and vinegar. Sprinkle with basil.

TIP FROM THE TEST KITCHEN
This salad is even more delicious served with dry, salty cheeses and crusty bread. Try it with a locally made sheep cheese and a rustic French-style boule or olive-studded ciabatta.

NUTRITIONAL INFORMATION, PER EACH OF 8 SERVINGS:
about 35 cal, 1 g pro, 2 g total fat (trace sat. fat), 4 g carb, 1 g fibre, 0 mg chol, 6 mg sodium. % RDI: 1% calcium, 2% iron, 9% vit A, 23% vit C, 8% folate.

Green Bean, Mushroom and Fennel Salad

HANDS-ON TIME	•	TOTAL TIME	•	MAKES
20 MINUTES		30 MINUTES		12 SERVINGS

What you need

⅓ cup	extra-virgin olive oil
¼ cup	lemon juice
3 tbsp	chopped fresh dill
1	clove garlic, minced
¾ tsp	salt
¼ tsp	pepper
450 g	small cremini mushrooms, quartered
450 g	green beans
half	bulb fennel, cored and thinly sliced

How to make it

In large bowl, whisk together oil, lemon juice, dill, garlic, salt and pepper. Add mushrooms and toss to coat. Let stand for 15 minutes, stirring occasionally.

Meanwhile, halve green beans diagonally. In saucepan of boiling water, blanch green beans until tender-crisp, 3 to 5 minutes. Using slotted spoon, transfer to bowl of ice water; let cool. Drain well; pat dry with towel.

Add beans and fennel to mushroom mixture; toss to coat. *(Make-ahead: Cover and refrigerate for up to 4 hours.)*

NUTRITIONAL INFORMATION, PER SERVING: about 76 cal, 2 g pro, 6 g total fat (1 g sat. fat), 5 g carb, 2 g fibre, 0 mg chol, 152 mg sodium, 262 mg potassium. % RDI: 2% calcium, 4% iron, 2% vit A, 10% vit C, 9% folate.

Waldorf Salad

HANDS-ON TIME	**TOTAL TIME**	**MAKES**
10 MINUTES	1¼ HOURS	6 TO 8 SERVINGS

What you need

1 cup	walnut halves
¼ cup	whipping cream (35%)
3 tbsp	mayonnaise (see tip, below)
1 tbsp	lemon juice
¼ tsp	each salt and pepper
1 cup	sliced celery
2	apples (Idared and/or Red Delicious), cored and sliced

How to make it

Spread walnut halves on rimmed baking sheet; toast in 350°F (180°C) oven until golden and fragrant, 6 to 8 minutes. Let cool. Coarsely chop; set aside.

In large bowl, whip cream until soft peaks form; fold in mayonnaise, lemon juice, salt and pepper.

Fold in walnuts, celery and apples. Refrigerate for 1 hour before serving.

TIP FROM THE TEST KITCHEN
Don't use light mayonnaise in this salad dressing. It adds a sweet-tart edge that detracts from the other flavours.

NUTRITIONAL INFORMATION, PER EACH OF 8 SERVINGS:
about 180 cal, 3 g pro, 16 g total fat (3 g sat. fat), 8 g carb, 2 g fibre, 12 mg chol, 116 mg sodium, 154 mg potassium. % RDI: 3% calcium, 4% iron, 4% vit A, 5% vit C, 10% folate.

Grilled Eggplant Salad

HANDS-ON TIME		TOTAL TIME		MAKES
25 MINUTES	•	2¼ HOURS	•	8 SERVINGS

What you need

2	eggplants (900 g total)
4	green onions, thinly sliced
¼ cup	chopped fresh parsley
¼ cup	chopped fresh cilantro
2	cloves garlic, minced
¼ cup	extra-virgin olive oil
2 tbsp	lemon juice
¾ tsp	salt
¼ tsp	pepper
3 tbsp	chopped walnuts (optional), toasted (see tip, page 119)

How to make it

Prick eggplants all over. Place on greased grill over medium-low heat or on rimmed baking sheet; close lid and grill or bake in 350°F (180°C) oven, turning often if on grill, until softened and charred, about 50 minutes. Let cool on plate.

Peel and discard skin and any juices from eggplants; coarsely chop flesh and transfer to serving bowl.

Stir in green onions, parsley, cilantro, garlic, oil, lemon juice, salt and pepper. Cover and refrigerate for 1 hour. *(Make-ahead: Refrigerate for up to 8 hours.)*

Just before serving, sprinkle with walnuts (if using).

TIP FROM THE TEST KITCHEN

This side is like a savoury fresh vegetable relish. Serve it with grilled meats; it's especially good with lamb.

NUTRITIONAL INFORMATION, PER SERVING: about 98 cal, 2 g pro, 7 g total fat (2 g sat. fat), 7 g carb, 2 g fibre, 0 mg chol, 217 mg sodium, 161 mg potassium. % RDI: 7% iron, 14% vit C, 7% folate.

Rainbow Veggie Salad

HANDS-ON TIME	•	TOTAL TIME	•	MAKES
15 MINUTES		35 MINUTES		4 SERVINGS

What you need

2 tbsp	olive oil
2 tbsp	vinegar or cider vinegar
1 tsp	liquid honey
¼ tsp	each salt and pepper
2 cups	thinly sliced red cabbage
1 cup	shredded carrot
1 cup	shredded zucchini
1 cup	bite-size broccoli florets
¼ cup	unsalted roasted sunflower seeds

How to make it

In bowl, stir together oil, vinegar, honey, salt and pepper until blended.

Add cabbage, carrot, zucchini, broccoli and sunflower seeds; toss to coat. Let stand for 20 minutes before serving. (*Make-ahead: Cover and refrigerate for up to 2 days.*)

TIP FROM THE TEST KITCHEN
This bright salad comes together a lot faster if you use a mandoline or the shredder blade on your food processor to shred the veggies.

NUTRITIONAL INFORMATION, PER SERVING: about 143 cal, 3 g pro, 11 g total fat (1 g sat. fat), 11 g carb, 3 g fibre, 0 mg chol, 32 mg sodium, 378 mg potassium. % RDI: 4% calcium, 6% iron, 39% vit A, 73% vit C, 25% folate.

Grapefruit and Fennel Salad

HANDS-ON TIME
15 MINUTES

•

TOTAL TIME
15 MINUTES

•

MAKES
6 TO 8 SERVINGS

What you need

1	ruby red grapefruit
4 cups	torn Bibb lettuce
2 cups	trimmed arugula, torn
2 cups	trimmed watercress
½ cup	thinly sliced cored fennel bulb

WHITE BALSAMIC AND MUSTARD DRESSING:

4 tsp	white balsamic vinegar
½ tsp	grainy mustard
¼ tsp	each salt and pepper
3 tbsp	canola or vegetable oil

How to make it

Peel grapefruit. Working over bowl, cut off outer membrane. Cut between membrane and pulp to release sections into bowl. Squeeze membranes to extract remaining juice. Remove 2 tbsp of the juice; set aside for dressing. Strain sections and set aside, saving any remaining juice for another purpose.

WHITE BALSAMIC AND MUSTARD DRESSING:
In large bowl, whisk together reserved grapefruit juice, vinegar, mustard, salt and pepper; slowly whisk in oil until emulsified.

Add lettuce, arugula, watercress and fennel to dressing; toss to coat. Garnish with reserved grapefruit sections.

NUTRITIONAL INFORMATION, PER EACH OF 8 SERVINGS:
about 67 cal, 1 g pro, 5 g total fat (trace sat. fat), 4 g carb, 1 g fibre,
0 mg chol, 88 mg sodium, 220 mg potassium. % RDI: 4% calcium,
3% iron, 11% vit A, 33% vit C, 18% folate.

Squash and Goat Cheese Salad

HANDS-ON TIME	•	TOTAL TIME	•	MAKES
30 MINUTES		1 HOUR		6 SERVINGS

What you need | How to make it

2	small squash (such as acorn or buttercup), each about 750 g
¼ cup	extra-virgin olive oil
3 tbsp	white balsamic vinegar or white wine vinegar
2 tbsp	vegetable oil
1 tsp	Dijon mustard
1	clove garlic, minced
¼ tsp	each salt and pepper
¼ tsp	dried thyme
pinch	granulated sugar
8 cups	mixed greens

CRISPY GOAT CHEESE:

1	log (300 g) soft goat cheese
1	egg
½ cup	panko or dried bread crumbs
¼ cup	minced fresh parsley
¼ tsp	each salt and pepper
2 tbsp	vegetable oil (approx)

Cut each squash in half; using spoon, scrape out seeds. Remove stems; cut each squash half crosswise into 6 half-moon slices, each about ½ inch (1 cm) thick, to make 24 pieces total. Place in large bowl; set aside.

Whisk together olive oil, vinegar, vegetable oil, mustard, garlic, salt, pepper, thyme and sugar. Add 3 tbsp of the oil mixture to squash, tossing to coat; place on foil-lined rimmed baking sheet. Roast in 375°F (190°C) oven, turning halfway through, until tender and golden, 30 minutes.

CRISPY GOAT CHEESE: Meanwhile, cut goat cheese into 12 slices; flatten slightly to make about 2½-inch (6 cm) rounds. In small bowl, whisk egg with 1 tsp water. In separate small bowl, toss together panko, parsley, salt and pepper. Dip cheese into egg, then panko mixture, pressing to coat. Place on parchment paper–lined rimmed baking sheet. *(Make-ahead: Cover and refrigerate squash and cheese separately for up to 6 hours.)*

In nonstick skillet, heat about 2 tbsp oil over medium heat; fry goat cheese, in batches, turning once and adding more oil if necessary, until crisp and golden, about 3 minutes. Drain on paper towel–lined plate.

In bowl, toss greens with remaining oil mixture; divide among 6 plates. Arrange 4 slices of the squash and 2 slices of the goat cheese around each salad.

NUTRITIONAL INFORMATION, PER SERVING: about 435 cal, 14 g pro, 30 g total fat (10 g sat. fat), 30 g carb, 4 g fibre, 54 mg chol, 487 mg sodium. % RDI: 18% calcium, 25% iron, 39% vit A, 45% vit C, 49% folate.

Shredded Brussels Sprout Salad

HANDS-ON TIME	•	TOTAL TIME	•	MAKES
20 MINUTES		30 MINUTES		4 SERVINGS

What you need

3 tbsp	light mayonnaise
2 tbsp	grated Parmesan cheese
1 tbsp	lemon juice
1 tsp	Dijon mustard
1 tsp	anchovy paste
1	large clove garlic, minced
½ tsp	Worcestershire sauce
pinch	pepper
4 cups	shredded brussels sprouts (about 16 sprouts), see tip, below
2 tbsp	extra-virgin olive oil
2 tbsp	diced prosciutto or bacon

How to make it

In large bowl, whisk together mayonnaise, Parmesan cheese, lemon juice, mustard, anchovy paste, garlic, Worcestershire sauce and pepper. Add brussels sprouts; toss to coat. Set aside.

In skillet, heat oil over medium heat; cook prosciutto until crisp. Add prosciutto with oil to sprouts mixture; toss to coat. Let stand until slightly wilted, about 10 minutes.

TIP FROM THE TEST KITCHEN
Brussels sprouts are too small to shred safely with a mandoline (you'll risk cutting your fingers). Instead, thinly slice them with a sharp chef's knife.

NUTRITIONAL INFORMATION, PER SERVING: about 160 cal, 5 g pro, 12 g total fat (2 g sat. fat), 10 g carb, 3 g fibre, 10 mg chol, 262 mg sodium. % RDI: 7% calcium, 11% iron, 9% vit A, 127% vit C, 25% folate.

Watermelon Salad

HANDS-ON TIME	•	TOTAL TIME	•	MAKES
10 MINUTES		10 MINUTES		4 SERVINGS

What you need | How to make it

1 tbsp	white wine vinegar
1 tbsp	extra-virgin olive oil
pinch	each salt and pepper
2 cups	seeded cubed watermelon
2 cups	diced cored fennel bulb
1	green onion, thinly sliced
2 tbsp	shaved Romano cheese (about 30 g), see tip, below

In large bowl, whisk together vinegar, oil, salt and pepper. Add watermelon, fennel and green onion. Toss gently to coat; top with Romano cheese.

TIP FROM THE TEST KITCHEN
Use a sharp vegetable peeler to shave pieces off the edge of a block of Romano cheese and into this salad.

NUTRITIONAL INFORMATION, PER SERVING: about 95 cal, 3 g pro, 6 g total fat (2 g sat. fat), 9 g carb, 2 g fibre, 7 mg chol, 109 mg sodium, 282 mg potassium. % RDI: 10% calcium, 4% iron, 6% vit A, 20% vit C, 8% folate.

Fruit Salad With Orange Syrup

HANDS-ON TIME
30 MINUTES

TOTAL TIME
1½ HOURS

MAKES
12 TO 16 SERVINGS

What you need

4	mangoes, peeled, pitted and chopped (see tip, page 150)
4	kiwifruit, peeled and chopped
half	cantaloupe, peeled, seeded and chopped
2 cups	green grapes, halved
1	pineapple, peeled, cored and chopped

ORANGE SYRUP:

1	orange
¼ cup	granulated sugar

How to make it

ORANGE SYRUP: Using vegetable peeler, peel zest off orange in strips; set aside. Halve orange; squeeze juice into glass measuring cup to make ⅓ cup. Set aside.

In small saucepan, bring sugar and ¼ cup water to boil over medium heat, stirring just until dissolved, about 1 minute. Remove from heat. Stir in orange zest; let stand for 10 minutes. Discard zest. Stir in reserved orange juice.

In large bowl, stir together mangoes, kiwifruit, cantaloupe, grapes and pineapple. Toss with orange syrup. Cover and refrigerate for 1 hour before serving. *(Make-ahead: Refrigerate for up to 8 hours.)*

NUTRITIONAL INFORMATION, PER EACH OF 16 SERVINGS: about 93 cal, 1 g pro, trace total fat (trace sat. fat), 24 g carb, 2 g fibre, 0 mg chol, 5 mg sodium, 266 mg potassium. % RDI: 2% calcium, 2% iron, 10% vit A, 88% vit C, 10% folate.

Grilled Fruit With Honeyed Crème Fraîche

HANDS-ON TIME	TOTAL TIME	MAKES
15 MINUTES	15 MINUTES	4 SERVINGS

What you need

2 tbsp	butter, melted
1 tbsp	bourbon
1 tbsp	liquid honey
4	small peaches, halved and pitted
4	rings fresh pineapple (½ inch/1 cm thick)
1	large mango, peeled, pitted and cut in large wedges (see tip, page 150)
2 tbsp	chopped fresh mint

HONEYED CRÈME FRAÎCHE:

¼ cup	crème fraîche
2 tsp	liquid honey
½ tsp	vanilla

How to make it

HONEYED CRÈME FRAÎCHE: Stir together crème fraîche, honey and vanilla. *(Make-ahead: Cover and refrigerate for up to 24 hours.)*

Stir together butter, bourbon and honey. Place peaches, pineapple and mango on greased grill over medium heat; close lid and grill, brushing with butter mixture and turning frequently, until softened and caramelized, about 5 minutes.

Arrange pineapple rings on 4 dessert plates; top with peaches and mango. Spoon crème fraîche mixture over top; sprinkle with mint.

TIP FROM THE TEST KITCHEN

For best results, use fruit that is ripe but still firm so it holds its shape on the grill. Anything too ripe may fall apart and slip through the grates.

NUTRITIONAL INFORMATION, PER SERVING: about 257 cal, 2 g pro, 12 g total fat (8 g sat. fat), 37 g carb, 4 g fibre, 40 mg chol, 49 mg sodium, 367 mg potassium. % RDI: 3% calcium, 6% iron, 22% vit A, 63% vit C, 7% folate.

Mango Melon Salad

HANDS-ON TIME	**TOTAL TIME**	**MAKES**
12 MINUTES	12 MINUTES	4 TO 6 SERVINGS

What you need

3 tbsp	lime juice
3 tbsp	liquid honey
2 cups	cubed (½ inch/1 cm) peeled pitted mango (see tip, below)
2 cups	cubed (½ inch/1 cm) peeled seeded cantaloupe
2 cups	cubed (½ inch/1 cm) peeled seedless watermelon
¼ cup	pine nuts (optional), toasted (see tip, page 97)
1 tbsp	thinly sliced fresh mint

How to make it

In large microwaveable bowl, stir lime juice with honey; microwave on high for 30 seconds. Whisk until honey is dissolved. Let cool.

Add mango, cantaloupe, watermelon, pine nuts (if using) and mint; toss to coat.

TIP FROM THE TEST KITCHEN

To prep a mango, cut off the stem end to make the bottom flat. Using a vegetable peeler, peel off half of the skin. Holding the peeled side with a paper towel to prevent slipping, peel the opposite side. Stand the mango on its flat bottom, and then cut the flesh off each wide side down to, but avoiding, the pit. Lay the slices on a cutting board and chop, slice or cube as needed.

NUTRITIONAL INFORMATION, PER EACH OF 6 SERVINGS:
about 103 cal, 1 g pro, trace total fat (trace sat. fat), 27 g carb, 2 g fibre, 0 mg chol, 12 mg sodium. % RDI: 2% calcium, 4% iron, 43% vit A, 65% vit C, 10% folate.

INDEX

◖ = Vegetarian

Index

🖤 = Vegetarian

Index

🍃 = Vegetarian

Index

Index

🍃 = Vegetarian

CREDITS

RECIPES

All recipes Tested Till Perfect by the Canadian Living Test Kitchen

PHOTOGRAPHY

RYAN BROOK p. 140.
JEFF COULSON back cover; p. 6, 9, 11, 14, 17, 24, 33, 44, 47, 48, 50, 55, 56, 61, 68, 71, 76, 84, 89, 99, 100, 103, 108, 111, 112, 117, 118, 122, 126, 129, 130 and 146.
YVONNE DUIVENVOORDEN front cover; p. 5, 18, 30, 37, 72, 75, 83, 94, 136 and 151.
JOE KIM p. 23 and 90.
EDWARD POND p. 34, 43, 62 and 135.
JODI PUDGE p. 143.
DAVID SCOTT p. 159.

FOOD STYLING

DAVID GRENIER p. 47, 76, 140 and 146.
ADELE HAGAN p. 33 and 50.
IAN MUGGRIDGE p. 143.
LUCIE RICHARD front cover; p. 5, 136, 151 and 159.
CLAIRE STUBBS p. 9, 18, 30, 37, 48, 55, 83, 94 and 135.
MELANIE STUPARYK p. 23, 44, 61 and 90.
NICOLE YOUNG back cover; p. 11, 14, 17, 24, 34, 43, 56, 62, 68, 71, 72, 75, 84, 89, 99, 100, 103, 108, 111, 112, 117, 118, 122, 126, 129 and 130.

PROP STYLING

LAURA BRANSON front cover; p. 33, 50, 136 and 143.
CATHERINE DOHERTY back cover; p. 6, 9, 11, 14, 17, 18, 24, 30, 47, 48, 56, 68, 71, 72, 75, 76, 83, 84, 89, 99, 100, 103, 108, 111, 112, 117, 118, 122, 126, 129, 130 and 146.
MADELEINE JOHARI 34, 43, 44, 55, 61 and 62.
KAREN KIRK p. 23, 90 and 140.
OKSANA SLAVUTYCH p. 5, 94, 135, 151 and 159.
GENEVIEVE WISEMAN p. 37.

Shredded Brussels
Sprout Salad
page 145

About Our Nutrition Information

To meet nutrient needs each day, moderately active women aged 25 to 49 need about 1,900 calories, 51 g protein, 261 g carbohydrate, 25 to 35 g fibre and not more than 63 g total fat (21 g saturated fat). Men and teenagers usually need more. Canadian sodium intake of approximately 3,500 mg daily should be reduced, whereas the intake of potassium from food sources should be increased to 4,700 mg per day. The percentage of recommended daily intake (% RDI) is based on the values used for Canadian food labels for calcium, iron, vitamins A and C, and folate.

Figures are rounded off. They are based on the first ingredient listed when there is a choice and do not include optional ingredients or those with no specified amounts.

ABBREVIATIONS
cal = calories
pro = protein
carb = carbohydrate
sat. fat = saturated fat
chol = cholesterol

Canadian Living

Complete your collection of Tested-Till-Perfect recipes!

The Ultimate Cookbook

The Complete Chicken Book
The Complete Chocolate Book
The Complete Preserving Book

400-Calorie Dinners
Dinner in 30 Minutes or Less
Essential Salads
Fish & Seafood
Make It Chocolate!
Pasta & Noodles
Sweet & Simple

New Slow Cooker Favourites

The Affordable Feasts Collection
The Appetizer Collection
The Barbecue Collection
The International Collection
The One Dish Collection
The Slow Cooker Collection
The Vegetarian Collection

150 Essential Beef, Pork & Lamb Recipes
150 Essential Salads
150 Essential Whole Grain Recipes

Available wherever books are sold or online at
canadianliving.com/books